A day may come when the courage
of men fails, when we forsake
our friends and break all bonds of
fellowship, but it is not this day.

An hour of woes and shattered
shields, when the age of men
comes crashing down!

But it is not this day!

This day we fight!

Aragorn, Lord of the Rings[1]

WHO IS READING *DARING*

Paul Cole is carrying one of the most important messages of our time, helping men discover their manhood and masculinity, something men everywhere are in desperate need of, in an increasingly feminized world. Any help we can give fathers and men generally to do life well together is vital, and by continuing the legacy of Dr. Ed Cole, Paul's father, Paul is giving the best of this help today.

~ **Phil Pringle**
Founder, Christian City Churches, Sydney

In *Daring: A Call to Courageous Manhood*, Paul Cole further expounds on the teachings of his late father, Dr. Ed Cole on what it means to maximize your manhood. He uses examples and quotations within this book that will awaken all men to rise up and take on the baton of leadership in our families and societies once again! Be prepared for some revelations in this book that will challenge, inspire and change your heart toward becoming the man that God intends us to be!

~ **Kong Hee**
Founder, City Harvest Church, Singapore

Paul Louis Cole has laid bare the secrets every man desires to know, how to be a daring and courageous man. With an innovative, fresh approach, *DARING* takes the wisdom of the ages and applies it to a man's life. God is moving around the world on the hearts of men, and let's not keep it quiet. My good friend Ed Cole, Paul's father, was one of the best examples of a man who dared to live by God's measure of manhood. The CMN ministry they founded builds men, not monuments. Ed's legacy has not only outlived him...it is powerfully alive and strong! I am pleased to encourage your partnering in this worthy endeavor.

~ **Pat Robertson**
Founder, CBN, Virginia Beach

As a pastor, I am so encouraged by the potential of Paul Cole's new book, *DARING: A Call to Courageous Manhood*, to call all men to begin living the lives God intended them to live. We are desperate today for Godly men to lead in our churches, our workplace and most certainly, our homes. I highly recommend this book to help you navigate the challenges of life to become God's man!

~ **Jonathan Falwell**
Pastor, Thomas Road Baptist Church, Lynchburg, Virginia

WHO IS READING *DARING*

DARING: A Call to Courageous Manhood is a fiery instrument at a strategic time. Pastoral leaders take this book in hand—get a copy for the men of your church—then lead them through it to ignite the renewed flame of practical, purposeful, manly living for this day!

~ Jack W. Hayford
Founding Pastor, The Church On The Way
President-Elect, The King's University
Los Angeles

I have often thought that the best handbook for men's ministry would be based on the camp-meeting song, "Dare to be a Daniel, Dare to stand alone! Dare to have a purpose firm! Dare to make it known." Paul Louis Cole has proven me right. *DARING: A Call to Courageous Manhood* masterfully bares the yearning heart of God for all sons of Adam, and electrifies the reader's heart to beat as loudly and strongly as the lion's heart of the tribe of Judah.

~ Leonard Sweet
Professor and NYT best-selling author,
Orcas Island

If your desire is to have Christ-loving, family-first, strong men of faith in your church, then I recommend you to Paul Cole. Men are transformed by the strong word Paul delivers. Paul has a huge heart to build strong local churches by building strong men!

~ Dino Rizzo
Lead Pastor, Healing Place Church, Louisiana

My brother, Paul, has written a masterpiece to challenge you to awake from complacency, defy your fears, and change your life. Reading *DARING*, you'll unearth the courage to live big for God and make a difference in our world!

~ Dale C. Bronner
Author and Founding Pastor,
Word of Faith Family Cathedral, Atlanta

PAUL LOUIS COLE

DARING

A CALL TO COURAGEOUS MANHOOD

WHITAKER
HOUSE

DARING:
A Call to Courageous Manhood

Christian Men's Network
P.O. Box 3
Grapevine, TX 76092
www.CMN.men
@ChristianMensNetwork
@EdwinLouisCole

ISBN: 978-1-64123-834-2
Printed in the United States of America
© 2014 Edwin and Nancy Cole Legacy LLC

Published by:
Whitaker House
1030 Hunt Valley Circle
New Kensington, PA 15068

This book has been printed digitally and produced in a standard specification in order to ensure its continuing availability.

APPRECIATION

To my extended family, sisters, cousins and loved ones who have given me the greatest gift a man can receive—your respect—I thank you, and I love you. To Joann, without whom there would be no book, you're amazing, I am indebted to you.

To my friends who have deeply impacted, enlarged, and enriched my life, I thank you. I love you. You are the shock absorbers of my life.

To the men of Hope Christian City Church, the men of the Christian Men's Network, to my Pastor Phil Pringle and the men of C3 Church International, all of whom have been my shelter and refuge, a source of strength and encouragement, I thank you. You are daring!

To my family, for whom I am now 'Papa,' I love you. Niles and Lindsay with Reese and Cameron, Brandon and Meredith, Bryce, I am so profoundly proud of you. You are God's gift to a man who never deserved so much. I am so grateful to be your Dad and Grandfather. You are all stunning.

To you, the daring one who has picked up this book, thank you for inviting me into your life. I pray your heart is encouraged.

CONTENTS

FOREWORD

Very few books have been forged through more blood sweat and tears than this powerful piece, aptly entitled **DARING**. It will inspire you to reach for greatness in your life. This remarkable book is a gift to the men of every nation!

With the explosion of growth in the ministry of the Christian Men's Network, I am humbled to partner with my friend, CMN President and author, Paul Louis Cole. Every time we are together, my life is expanded, energized and encouraged. Paul's message is challenging, but is undercut with encouragement that emboldens the reader to aspire higher, and take life to the next level.

I thank God for placing the thought of the men's movement in the heart of my friend Ed Cole, and for his son Paul, who is carrying the mantle onward. The enormity of his sacrifice personally to sustain the spectacular treasure called "Christian Men's Network" is incalculable. I have seen firsthand the price paid. It has been staggering! To say that Paul is personally a daring man is a profound understatement.

To embrace the words of **DARING** is to be revolutionized! This is a book of transformation and courage, with a fresh, relevant, pertinent message for all men around the world. Paul's dad at age 79 had men in their 20's, 30's and 40's clamoring to be like him. Paul has that same quality to draw men to him, as a "brother," and yet to challenge us all to live as courageous men—the men God designed us to be!

~ Dr. Jim Garlow
NYT bestselling author and Senior Pastor of Skyline Church, San Diego
Chairman, Renewing American Leadership, Washington, DC

In the obscure hills of the southern Sinai desert it's another hot, crushingly dense late afternoon. Death has etched a jagged outline of pain into the graying dust-tinged atmosphere.

The leader, the general, the rescuer is down. Moses is dead, gone, part of the past. Now, his assistant, Joshua, has to stand and lead. He grimaces as he surveys the land ahead and the multitude of people before him, his face a mirror of the wind-ravaged wilderness. It's painfully apparent in his eyes that he's not sure he's up to the task. He looks to his friends of eighty years. They tell him, "Take courage!"

Needing wisdom from God, he looks to the heavens. The word of instruction from God: "Take courage."

He looks to the crowds around him. They say: "Joshua, take courage!" How does he do that? We're about to find out.

The same encouragement is echoed through the ages to men who would be leaders:

> **"Take courage."**

Paul the apostle repeats the same command to leaders this way:

> **"Keep alert. Be firm in your faith.**
> **Stay brave and strong."**
>
> (1 Corinthians 16:13, CEV)

Another translation of Paul's charge to leaders includes:

> **"Act like men and be courageous"** (AMP)

Paul expects real men to have guts, endurance, fortitude, strength, and a heart to fight. We all want that. It's expected. We must be these men—men who will confront the enemy, face the firestorms of tribulation, be willing to sacrifice for victory, stand against evil, fight for the next generation, and hold nothing back.

When the pain of betrayal strikes, finances are tight, or the day (or week, or month) is not going right... When pressure brings dark thoughts, the way out is blocked, and joy is a distant memory... When freedom is just a word... When all around us falls the debris of failure, that is when daring men stand strong. That is when we fight. That is when we are men on our guard.

It's a fight to be resolute in our faith in God, to embrace the truth that He is really there. We battle to fill our hearts and minds with His Word, to be filled with courage and strength. This is when we fight the sacred fight of men...

This is when we face the true test—the fiery crucible of character.

This is when we must...

...act like a man.

INTRODUCTION

"Act like a man"?

What does that look like? When do I get there? What do I wear? Who are my friends? How much do I have to make? What kind of house do I need to have? Do I have to be traditional? When do I get to that place where I look like a real man?

There is no gray turmoil in the Bible's definition of what a real man looks like. A REAL MAN looks like Jesus Christ. Done. No discussion. That's it.

So how does that play out in real life? In MY life? Maturity is one part, another is loving people, another is being a man of integrity, and yet more would be helping others, being unselfish, and giving generously. Perhaps one area we overlook more than any: Jesus was a DARING man. He was bold, resolute, unyielding, strong, powerful, and focused.

So, let's take DARING. If we're going to do at least one thing, *let's do that one.*

Be daring!

Not the extreme skier, climber of skyscrapers, or hydroplane racer...

The man who would be daring is defined first by an inner strength manifested in an outward expression. Personal philosophy determines public performance. Daring is first internal before it is external.

Daring: to confront boldly and courageously, willing to risk, fearless.

The daring man is the man who faces life, enemy, culture, and obstacles with a spirit that is both bold and courageous. Daring comes through the empowering grace of God in the heart of a man.

DARING MEN STAND 1

WAR

Cream blaring from the radio, windows open, long hair blowing. We're blasting the song "Sunshine of Your Love" in a two-hour maniacal repetition of a four-minute song.

Casey and I are in my forty-horsepower Volkswagen bus headed to San Francisco. No bumpers. No first gear. Surfboards are on top and with a couple good tires, we're on our way to the groovin' hippie Haight-Ashbury scene.

It's 1968.

The Vietnam War is hot, and antiwar protests seem to be on every corner. Most of the colleges are at varying stages of being shut down because of the demonstrations and the streets are filled with mayhem.

War in Vietnam has filled the news since junior high. Before that, we were hiding under desks in safety drills, believing at any minute the Communists were about to drop a bomb right on my little town of Chico, California.

War in Southeast Asia in the 1960s was a painful era, but no less than the pain families have endured when their sons and daughters didn't come home from Somalia, Korea, Yemen, Iraq, Afghanistan, or other battle-torn areas.

I was born during the Korean War, lost my friends during the Vietnam War and global conflict has filled the news my entire life.

War and conflict seem to be an inevitable sequence in the flow of the earth. The reality is that conflict is all around us. The Bible says there are wars in the supernatural continuously, so it's part of life as a follower of Christ.

There is a "take-no-prisoners" eternal battle happening. We were all born into the middle of it.

No matter what year you were born or on what continent, you arrived in the middle of a war.

You have two choices:
Engage the enemy, or run.
Fight, or surrender.
Face life, or float in the random winds of chance.

So how do we get the guts to fight? Where does that inner resource come from? What is the process to become a warrior, a man of daring—a man who will grow up beyond those boyhood experiments and not run in the times of trouble?

Considered one of the most courageous U.S. presidents, Theodore Roosevelt said, "It is only through labor and painful effort, by grim energy and resolute courage, that we move on to better things."[3] Courage arrives in the sweat of facing our inner fears.

The people who fight best in life are not the smartest, strongest, most brilliant, or most talented. They are simply those who will not quit, who tenaciously grip the sword of faith with endurance, guts, and a resolute spirit.

They believe their life has purpose and meaning, that a divine destiny lies before them, and that their destiny is

something worth

fighting

for!

Courage is the result of embraced destiny.

Let's start by putting a context on our discussion...

What is your reaction to this statement?

The level of life I am now living on,
is not at the full capacity of my life.

☐ Yes
or
☐ No

What jumps up in your heart? Think about that... is there more?

Do you sense that life should be larger? That there's a higher level of living? A place that's closer to God? A level of life that has greater strength, deeper insight, healthier emotional levels, more power, or firmer resolve?

This book is about going there.

It's about creating a vibrant, powerful new level of strength in our hearts—a place we know we can go to but seldom succeed in accessing. This is about going where we know we've always wanted to be, to become,

A Daring Man.

"One man with courage makes a majority."[4]

– Andrew Jackson

Did he make this wave?
Did he wipe out?

If you knew the chances were you would crash and wipeout, would you still take off?

Is there something inside you that says, "Let's at least give it a try," because there's a chance you *would* make it? Or, has life taught you that you shouldn't attempt what seems impossible?

Perhaps the real tragedy of life is never knowing.

> *Pain is temporary. It may last a minute, or an hour, or a day, or a year, but eventually it will subside and something else will take its place. If I quit, however, it lasts forever.*[5]

> ~ Lance Armstrong

Daring is an attitude.
It starts in your heart,
and flows to your hands.

Three Teens

The dawning sun slices a jagged opening in the purple-orange haze draped like southern moss across the tops of distant rock-strewn hills that surround the warming desert plains north of Damascus. It's the day of the decree.

In the middle of a million gathered people, three men stand unnoticed in the dusty throng. They're about to be on the wrong side of a new law—one that will engulf them in a legal sentence casting them to a grisly death.

It's a well-known story. A king gets his ego bruised. Evil men with hidden agendas lead him to make a decree that will expose those who are followers of Jehovah God.

The king, Nebuchadnezzar, builds a large monument, a solid gold ninety-foot-tall image of himself, puts it in the middle of a massive desert plain, and commands millions to come to worship the idol, thus professing their commitment to him as the king. To refuse is a cruel death.

Three friends in their late teens—Shadrach, Meshach and Abednego—cannot bow to the idol and also keep the commandments of their God.

The music plays, a million people hit the ground in flat-out prostrated worship.

These three men stand.

They can be seen for miles. There's the ninety-foot idol, and there's the three of them.

The king orders the law to be upheld.

"Burn them!"

The three men are thrown in furnaces so hot that men standing near the entrances are killed by the heat.

They didn't have a committee meeting. They didn't wave Bibles or placards. They didn't have their own TV show or do radio interviews. In the face of evil, they simply stood when all others bowed. A staggeringly simple strategy:

When all others bow... stand.

It was not easy, it wasn't without fear or misgivings or sweat or a quick, furtive look at each other or an anxious breath...

It was just the right thing to do, and that's what they did—the right thing.

Doing the right thing is not always the easiest thing, but it's always the right thing.

The Son of God showed up in the fire, saved their lives, and walked them out of the furnace and into their destiny. They became leaders in the nation. The three teens didn't set out to prove something, to be heroes, or to be brave. They weren't even planning to become great leaders. They were planning to be dead. They just simply believed in the Word of God, made a commitment, and stuck to it.

When all others bow... stand.

"Champions are men in whom courage has become visible."[6]

~ Edwin Louis Cole

Daring men stand, but they don't stand still

Some make much of Jesus never owning a house, most often in the context of a pious applaud to poverty. It is without any basis. If Jesus were impoverished, why did He need a full-time treasurer in Judas, the keeper of the money? But that's beside the point.

Jesus *did* have a house—His dad's. Like other young men in Israel, he most likely built an apartment onto his dad's place and stayed there until he left home at the age of thirty. From that point on, He never needed a house. He was never home. He was in motion! He spent much time in Bethany at Lazarus' house. He was often at other friends' homes. But once He set out, He was a man on the move.

Men pray for direction in life, but the only man who needs direction is the one who is going somewhere. Abraham set out for a land. He wasn't sure where it was, but he knew it wasn't where he was standing at that moment. It was time to move. Just start!

Daring men move. Take a step forward in faith. *Let's go!*

Proverbs says a working ox will make a stall dirty, but without the dirt, there's no profit. When work is happening, stuff gets dirty. Dusty roads will soil your jacket, and you'll have to clean your bike's filters. But the dirt is proof you're moving.

As my friend Robert asks often, "What part of the word *go* do you not understand?"

Daring men start.
Daring men get dirty.

Passion, energy, character, focus, daring, and just sheer guts—those are the most important parts of a winning plan. Strategy is nothing without men who have that.

"If you don't have blood on your kilt, then you're just a dancer."[8]

- Old Scottish proverb

"It is not the critic who counts: not the man who points out how the strong man stumbles or where the doer of deeds could have done better. The credit belongs to the man who is actually in the arena, whose face is marred by dust and sweat and blood, who strives valiantly, who errs and comes up short again and again, because there is no effort without error or shortcoming, but who knows the great enthusiasms, the great devotions, who spends himself for a worthy cause; who, at the best, knows, in the end, the triumph of high achievement, and who, at the worst, if he fails, at least he fails while daring greatly, so that his place shall never be with those cold and timid souls who knew neither victory nor defeat."[7]

~Theodore Roosevelt

The Crisis of Daring Men

You watched the video. You went to the meetings. You got the book. You tried to copy what you saw. Yet still, the eye of the hurricane is hanging over you like a storm from hell, and it's not moving any time soon.

Manhood is in crisis across the globe.

The bedrock truths of this vibrant garden planet where daring men once fought wild animals by hand, carved cultures out of the dirt, triumphed over the unknown seas, and tamed the rugged territories are now scattered like the pillaged ruins of Carthage from floods of unfaithfulness, tsunamis of greed, earthquakes of integrity, and the cratering remnants of hollow character.

Toxic shadows fall across the great granite cathedrals, castles, and courts of the world. The ghost of real manhood has limped away with the fallen heroes. The era of chivalry died with them. The time of the statesman passed. The annals of the warriors closed. The pages of the pioneers decayed. And the days when a man's word was his bond have drifted listlessly down the meandering rivers of mediocrity.

Yet, from the distant hills, comes the rising sound of a new day, legions of daring men reclaiming the rights to real manhood. Today's Shadrachs. Today's Meshachs. Today's Abednegos. Planting their stake in masculinity, refusing the stereotype that manliness is synonymous with being a jerk, they are forging a present-day model for manhood, where Christlikeness is the standard, their word is the measure of their character, and the stewardship of their relationships is considered priority over toys, tarts, or trifles.

And so now comes the really hard question:
Are you willing to do what it takes to be a daring man?
Do you want in?

You can challenge culture and change the course of history.

It will be hard and will take more guts and determination than you think you have. The pain will often hurt to your bones. It may not make you popular. Some may misunderstand you. Others may cuss you. Religious people may think you've gone overboard. Death may be the only prize and the jungles ahead of your path may be crammed with all that is poisonous.

But, here's the takeaway, the result of becoming daring: daring men are transforming cultures around the world. They're doing the difficult and impossible, facing down the giants of greed, the pornmongers, the purveyors of sleeze, the virulent vultures of human trafficking, going up against the bastilles of God-slandering theological institutions, tearing down the barriers of prejudice, and loudly declaring a new day.

This is the day for godly daring men!

Daring men are rebuilding the foundations brick by brick, from politics to the judicial system, corporate business, small business, broadcast media, sports, music, athletics, the arts and every aspect of culture.

A mind-set of truth, honor, and integrity is gaining momentum to replace the current world order in which men can flagrantly break societal rules then litigate when they are faced with the penalties. Entertainers, divorced dads, business professionals, and even some ministers squirm their way out of the consequences of their actions instead of facing them like men.

Let's bring back the backbone of masculinity!

If everyone thinks they are the exception, then the exception *is* the rule, and we've lost the standard. The standard of a daring man is that manhood and Christlikeness are synonymous. Simply put, to be a real man, we model our manhood on the greatest man who ever walked the earth. That's it and we're done.

Our model is Jesus Christ. Period. Not the ancient artist's weak, silky-skinned Jesus with the tousled hair and penchant for picking up children and sheep. The real Jesus! The Man with the weather-lined face of the outdoorsman, the tough feet of the trekker, the hardened body of the lumber worker, and the penetrating eyes of the One who knows people... and cares.

It starts with relationships—first our relationship to God, then our relationship with others, all held together by the integrity of our hearts. By developing a solid core in our relationship with Christ, our God-given manhood is foundationally established, our integrity grounded.

Since Adam, men have identified themselves by their professions, hobbies, skills, passions, gifts, money, position of power, popularity and more...but, none of these are the true foundation of manhood.

In a world shaken by spiraling personal debt, corrupted financial systems, city, state, and national economies failing, it seems harder than ever to accept responsibility and engage the courage required to measure our hearts and move forward. Daring men cannot accept the philosophy of a failed culture. If we accept the philosophy, we accept the failure. The day of only appearing to be men of character is over, the posing is dead—we have to be who we *really* are.

Real men today are calling it like it is. Those who grab the new standard of daring men make relationships to family and friends a priority. God put us on the planet to live in relationship. Our approach to marriage and family gets rethought when we accept the standard of God's Word. The simple truth is that more children are birthed out of marriage than ever before, divorce seems unstoppable, and the institution of marriage itself has been attacked by the enemies of God—with no sign of abating. Daring men recognize that marriage was created by God between a man and woman to reflect the biblical relationship between Christ, the groom, and the church, His bride. As such, it can be the closest thing to heaven or hell we will ever experience on this earth. We choose heaven.

It's time for a new call to godly manhood. Strong, unashamed, and bold.

We've been in the trap. We've seen what we believed in crumble and corrode. It's time for a call to the eternal standards of truth.

**Men and nations are not great
by virtue of their wealth,
but by the wealth of their virtue.**

~ Edwin Louis Cole

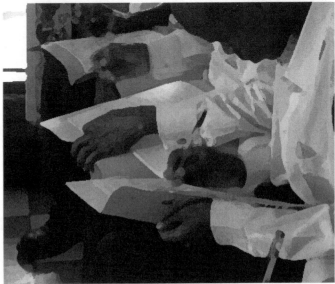

We may have great crowds with great sermons, but we will never change a nation until we disciple a man.

Daring men will change the future, and it starts now.

The Lodgepole Pine

There's a majestic pine tree that grows tall and straight, up in the high mountains of the western U.S. I climbed there often as a kid and return when I can to get the fresh, invigorating spirit of the spectacular, picturesque heights.

Starting at around the 6,000-foot elevation and continuing to the filtering edges of the timberline is a stately pine tree called the "lodgepole pine." This strong tree was named for its use by first-nation people to anchor the center of their homes, the teepee. Later it was used for telephone poles and railroad ties. It grows strong and straight, 70 to 80 feet tall. Its dense groves of unparalleled natural beauty canopy the breathtaking snow-lined peaks.

What is unique is how it reproduces. Pine trees produce their seeds in a pod, the pinecone. A series of seeds are embedded in a cone-shaped pod that falls off the tree, and expels the seeds from the cone onto the ground. The lodgepole pinecone is different. The lodgepole pinecone is covered by a type of resin shield called "pitch," a serotinous shroud. When the pinecone falls onto the floor of the forest, it sits there, the seeds held inside the pitch. Many lodgepole pinecones will stay on the trees or on the ground unopened for dozens of years.

The only element that will open the lodgepole pinecone and allow the seeds to be spread for new trees and life in the forest is fire or extreme heat.

When forest fires rage through the gorgeous mountains, it is seen by most as tragic destruction. The trees, the grandeur of the forests, marred! Except for the lodgepole pine. Because it is when the fires come, the seeds are released and life is renewed.

The seeds of life are released only when the heat of the fire opens the cone.

The same is true in our lives. What may look like destruction can actually be the force, or fire, that thrusts us to our next level of life.

We can say with confidence...

The seeds of success are sown in the fires of adversity.

Jesus said, "In this world you will have obstacles, troubles, trials, and the fires of adversity, but take heart for I have overcome the world" (John 16:33, my paraphrase). He teaches and shows by example that in our greatest testing is where we find our greatest strength. When you look at the lives of the truly great, you realize what they have in common—a great obstacle. If it weren't for the adversity, they wouldn't have been known as a champion. Think of it!

Kelly Slater, both the youngest and now oldest champion in surfing history, is great because he does the unimaginable by pitting himself against the power of the ocean and catching and taming the impossible waves that others cannot.

Dick Hoyt is not the greatest triathlete in the world, but he is one of the most famous and fulfilled because he competes in all three events while pulling or carrying his son, Rick, a quadriplegic.

Franklin Delano Roosevelt, faced with an unwinnable war against unspeakable evil announced the U.S. would become the "Arsenal of Democracy." He called for the impossible task of creating airplanes to take the war to the skies. He won the war when the people he inspired created

not six thousand planes per year as in the past, but in five years, built three hundred thousand war planes.

When we don't have the challenges, disasters, losses, failures, and attacks and when we are coasting instead of being accosted by the lawsuits, betrayals, and disappointments of a war-ravaged life, we do not develop the strength of mind and heart necessary to become a true champion, a man of daring.

It is not when things are going right that we look for a savior. But in the fires of life, we find our life in Christ!

> *Jesus answered them…"The Father is with me. I've told you all this so that **trusting me, you will be unshakable** and assured, deeply at peace. In this godless world you will continue to experience difficulties. But take heart! I've conquered the world."*
>
> *~ John 16:31–33, THE MESSAGE, emphasis added*

"Faith is a living, daring confidence in God's grace, so sure and certain that a man could stake his life on it a thousand times."[9]

- Martin Luther

DARING MEN FOLLOW GOD

Daring Men Hear Christ

A dirty sidestreet of Lima, Peru, young missionary Robert Barriger is waiting at the post office as he did every Friday. Weekly checks from America brought money for food—not for him, but for the dozens of orphans in the shelter he'd built in the mountains.

At the orphanage, it's tense. Shining Path guerillas have surrounded the gated entrance, expecting the gringo missionary to come with money, as he did every Friday. They have cased the place and chosen their time to attack.

Robert waits unknowing the danger, the guerrillas wait knowing their target, the staff at the orphanage are terrified.

Down in the town, the postman arrives. No letters. No money. Robert is devastated, he has no food for the kids. He decides to wait for the afternoon mail. The guerrillas are impatient, yelling threats at the workers in the compound.

Robert never saw this day coming. Growing up a surfer in Huntington Beach, California, living at the ocean, partying and enjoying the lifestyle of wild youth, being hunted by terrorists was not in the plan.

A few years earlier, he'd been living in a sandy,

cramped garage with Mexican rugs strewn on concrete floors, dirty pillows layered over discarded mattresses, surfboards stacked in every available space, the salt air from the nearby ocean mixed with the odor of unkempt men, and the acrid aroma of marijuana smoke hanging in the air—lost boys in a fatherless spin.

His counselor at school had told him, "You'll never do anything good in life. You'll never do anything but end up in prison." So he quit and pursued the perfect wave. But a Christian grandma, an old lady in their eyes, saw the daring young surfers, made them her target and one young man listened.

Robert's biggest challenge was to believe someone really loved him. Finally convinced, he surrendered to Christ and gave himself totally and completely to serve the Lord.

What happens when a daring, all-out surfer finds Christ? He wants to be all-out daring for God. He heads to ministry school, meets a beautiful girl from an equally turbulent background, and they go out street witnessing on their first date.

Again, a professor looks at his surfer roots and heart for the "daring" part of life and tells him, "You're not cut out for ministry. You'll never lead. You're too wild."

Robert and Karyn marry and become missionaries because he's told it's the hardest thing someone can do to show their love for Christ. With two babies in arms, the young couple scrapes together enough money to buy one-way tickets to the jungles of Peru then do whatever it takes to lead people to Christ. The daring nature of the "wild" surfer is exactly what it will take to push through the obstacles of jungle terrorists and institutional indifference. That includes taking in native children to protect them from pervasive terrorists.

Now, they're about to kill him.

At the end of the day, no money has arrived. Robert has to walk, bus, and hitchhike to get to the kids to tell them there will be no food today. His heart weighs down toward his empty stomach, the delays just getting out to the orphanage are excruciating to his emotions. No cell phones. No communication. He has no idea what his kids and staff have endured while he waited in town.

Robert is shocked when he knocks on the door and the staff screams, "Pastor Robert, you're alive!" Hugs and tears. They tell him what happened. The guerrillas waited all day to ambush Robert, but got bored as Robert waited in town for the mail that never came. Having no mail arrive saved Robert's life.

That was the only week money didn't arrive in the mail. The next week, Robert was back at the post office and went back to the shelter with money for food.

Since the miracle of "no mail," Robert and Karyn Barriger have built an enormous ministry to the hurting and marginalized of Peru. Against pervasive odds and negative setbacks, their ministry has thrived. People from nations across the world come to see the model of what God has done through their ministry. Millions of children have received help, thousands attend their churches, and the lost surfer from the garage has seen God begin the transformation of a nation.

Daring men don't listen to negative talk. They are daring men.

Daring Men Hold Nothing Back

Paul wrote to his guys in Acts 20. He said, "When I was there with you, I taught you in public and in private. I gave you everything you need to be successful...I HELD NOTHING BACK."

Athletes engaged in competition often say, "I left it all on the field." It means they held nothing in reserve. They gave it all for the game. Whether in defeat or victory, there was nothing held back.

Paul accomplished prodigious amounts of work by holding nothing back. The principle is to leave it all on the field. It's the mark of a tenacious, daring, generous spirit. It is the character of Almighty God, that He gave ALL. He gave His Son Jesus for the redemption and transformation of mankind. There was no plan B, no "hold back a little in case this doesn't work." It was ALL on the line.

Standing on a steep mountain slope with Jim Hunter, downhill ski champion of Canada, Olympic medalist, and extreme skier, I asked Jim, "How can you do 80 miles per hour (130 km/h) down a mountain on snow that's been purposely iced, hard as rock, and not worry that at any moment you could fall, be hurt badly, paralyzed, career over. How do you do that?"

Jim replied, "I focus on the finish, and ski with reckless abandon."

The daring man is focused forward, and holds nothing back.

Joshua: Daring Man with a Big God

Joshua is having some difficult days. He's surrounded by enemy armies. He's dealing with huge problems and everyone's looking to him for answers.

Joshua is the leader of Israel that takes them into the Promised Land, their place of destiny. Moses is dead, and Joshua is in command...but every step seems painful, filled with war and terror, grumbling people and confusing directions, deadly nights and searingly hot days. Ever felt like Joshua?

Here's an answer we can trust in:

God is having a good day. He never had a bad one. He never woke up with that sinking feeling. He's never been unsuccessful. He's never had an unsuccessful thought. He's never said, "Bummer, that didn't work."

God is a God of wisdom. Wisdom produces strategy. We need a wise strategy to fight for victory. According to Scripture, the first thing God ever created was not the universe, the earth, or day and night. It was wisdom (Proverbs 8:22–23, 30). Wisdom became the "architect" of everything that exists. So, for victory in our lives, we need wisdom!

We can have wisdom. James wrote, "If a man needs wisdom, let him ask the Lord, who will give it to him without hesitation" (James 1:5). We don't have to qualify for wisdom or go to the right school. I've met some Oxford grads without any wisdom. We don't have to be the head of a company or leader of some group. ANYONE who asks God for wisdom will get it. Now, right now, ask. Go ahead—get some wisdom. It's free, never runs out, and is available in endless supply every time you ask for it.

Wisdom is the application of understanding and knowledge. Knowing the right thing to do is not as important as knowing when to do it. Doing the right thing is more important than doing things right. God desires that we would have wisdom to do the right thing at the right time.

The apostle Paul wrote to his young protégé Timothy over and over, "Stir up the gift that is in you" (2 Timothy 1:6, my paraphrase). "Don't let people intimidate you." "Don't worry about being young." "Don't worry about small beginnings." Then he said: "For God did not give us a spirit of timidity, but a spirit of power, of love and of self-discipline" (2 Timothy 1:7, NIV). Paul knew that Timothy could be intimidated, so he said, in essence, "God gave you the power and the anointing of the Holy Spirit, not a spirit of fear but of power, love, and a sound mind." A sound mind means wise judgment.

God gives us wisdom. Wisdom is the ability to do the right thing at the right time in the right way.

Joshua is a man in whom wisdom became evident. His strategy and decisions run the razor edge of genius. That is the path of every wise man covered by the powerful presence of Almighty God.

Joshua is now the general of a major army and the leader of an entire nation. He's trained for it. He's been faithfully serving others, working hard, building his character, and now he's there. Moses is dead. Joshua is now the man.

Only problem: there are thousands of powerful enemies surrounding them. They've been traveling for years without getting anywhere. The famous, trusted and beloved leader is dead and Joshua needs a plan! *Some wisdom gotta drop down right here, right now, God!*

God's plans are always for our success.

"For I know the plans I have for you," says the LORD. *"They are plans for good and not for disaster, to give you a future and a hope"* (Jeremiah 29:11).

In these words, God is intent on not being misunderstood. People are thinking, "He's not on top of things, not planning right. He's slipping up and somehow is out of touch with things on earth."

Ever been misunderstood?
Ever thought God has forgotten you?

Here, God spells it out: "For I know the plans I have for you..." God writes, to you, "I know what I'm thinking." Even if no one else knows, God knows.

He states it strongly, an emphasis of consternation, "*I know* the thoughts I have for you!" So often we let others tell us what God is thinking, what He's like, and how He operates. Here, God says, "TIME OUT! I KNOW! The dreams, plans and desires I have for you—*I KNOW!*"

In those words are the implication that we've been listening to the wrong voices. It's like a contrast and compare, but it's part X without part Y, because part Y is understood. "I KNOW!" He says and by saying so, He infers part Y, which is, *"THEY DON'T KNOW!"*

We let others rip us off. *They don't know.* YOU don't even always know! But, God knows. And, He'll tell you.

God KNOWS!

Here's what God wrote about us: "For we are God's masterpiece, He has created us anew in Christ Jesus, so that we can do the good things He planned for us long ago...." (Ephesians 2:10, NLT).

GOD KNOWS, THEY DON'T KNOW!

God always wins. And He is for us, not against us. He is on OUR side, we are on HIS side, and HE never loses.

God never ends anything on a negative. Negativity is transitory. It's something we go through to get to somewhere else. It's not the end. It's just a means to get to the end.

The world says, "You win some. You lose some."

The world says, "You can't win them all."

God wins them all.

God has always been successful. We're tapped into THAT!

Teddy Roosevelt said, "You cannot fight hard, unless you believe you are fighting to win."[11]

Michelangelo said, "The greatest danger for us all is not that our goals are too high and we miss them, but that they are too low and we reach them."[12]

In the movie *The Truman Show*, the character "Christof" played by Ed Harris, said, "We accept the reality of the world with which we are presented."[13]

Jesus won the victory over hell, Satan, and death. He was and is a champion, a winner, and the ultimate daring Man.

Wisdom empowers us to step into THAT world.

The world of a daring conqueror!

Daring Men Plan to Win

Joshua and the people of Israel were brought back to the Jordan to a place of fear and defeat, but only so they could become successful. Ever wonder why you keep going through the same test of life? It's so you can ultimately win. It's not punishment.

God wants you to win. He brings you back to the same test in His mercy, so that you can finally beat it. Arriving at the same obstacle over and over is not God's masochistic, penurious bent. It's His grace. It's Him saying to you, "You will win!"

You will succeed. You will fight and battle, in His strength, until you do.

Make plans to win. God does.

So often God is misunderstood. "The truth is," Christ says, "anyone who believes in Me will do the same works I have done, and even greater works, because I am going to be with the Father. You can ask for anything in my name and I will do it, because the work of the Son brings glory to the Father" (John 14:12–13, my paraphrase). Mustering the courage to overcome adversity, we work at, but do we have the daring to embrace GREATER WORKS than Jesus? Coming out of our hands? God says we'll do it, and we'll succeed.

"Little children, you are of God [you belong to Him] and have [already] defeated and overcome them [the agents of the antichrist], because he Who lives in you is greater (mightier) than he who is in the world" (1 John 4:4, AMP). Courage is the result of embraced destiny. It starts in your heart and flows through your hands.

God's destiny for you is success.

With Moses gone, Joshua committed himself whole-heartedly to following God. Surrounded by powerful enemies, he didn't panic...he trusted God. Confident of God's heart, he embraced God's plans. His decision to be faithful to the Word of God brought him wisdom and strength of spirit.

Faithfulness made Joshua a great leader...

God's wisdom made him a great conqueror.

"Yes, risk-taking is inherently failure-prone.

Otherwise, it would be called sure-thing-taking."[15]

- Jim McMahon, pro football player

DARING MEN ARE FIGHTERS

Daring Men Are Connected

Joshua is a warrior. He is a daring man. Second in command to Moses, he's in charge of military strategy and tasked with defeating the enemy. Nothing must stand in the way of the nation's destiny. But, because of the sin of Israel, not his sin, they're all stuck in the desert. Within striking distance of Canaan, the Promised Land, they're wandering.

Joshua has been there. As one of Moses' spies, he'd been to the Promised Land. He's seen it. Moses hasn't. Liberated from the dust of desert treks, Joshua has inhaled the aroma of a fertile soil. Delivered from the diet of daily manna, he's tasted the sweetness of giant grapes. Unconstrained by the unyielding barrenness of the wilderness, he's looked across panoramic plains and hiked majestic mountains.

Joshua knows the way and knows what he's missing.

Yet, he's following a path that takes him away, then closer, then away, then closer. Why did he not take a group of warriors and families and just leave? Why not just get there? Why not split the nation and go his way?

Joshua was loyal. He was loyal to Moses and faithful to the vision that God had given through Moses. Out of honor, he stayed. And, because of his loyalty and being faithful, he became the leader of the nation.

Blessing Follows Honor

The Psalmist wrote, "Those who are planted in the house will flourish" (Psalm 92:1, my paraphrase). This is a principle for you and me today. It's a principle of battle—STAY CONNECTED.

Disconnection leads to dislocation, dysfunction, and death.

What is not connected will not grow.

We live in an instant culture. We want it now. Many men have chafed under the correction of the leader, the direction of the boss, and the tutelage of a spiritual mentor. Then, out of frustration, they set out on their own business or ministry without the blessing that honor and loyalty would have brought them. They may bloom for a season, but it is not a long-term solution.

Stay connected.

A wise man saw a sculptor at work. The artist struck his hammer on the stone. He chipped and chipped at the stone. Finally, a brilliant statue emerged. The observer wondered, which was the most important strike of the hammer? The last, which revealed the completed beautiful work, or the first, which began it? Perhaps it was the continued striking of the hammer, the sweat that showed endurance, fortitude, and passion.

What creates the finished product is not always a brilliant concept or the skill of the artist. It's the constancy of the hammer. Still working when the days have become long and hard, still moving when the end result seems far away.

Daring men have the guts to press on when vision is still just a dream in the heart.

Persistence wins battles.

Being connected wins the war.

Daring Men Hang Out With Daring Men

To keep company with daring men is to see what it takes to become a daring man...to sense the inner resolve that daring men possess. Find daring men and hang out with them. Let their spirit touch your life.

Just as iron sharpens iron, friends sharpen the minds of each other.
~ Proverbs 27:17, CEV

If you want to increase your record of success, hang out with successful men. To become a better golfer, play golf with someone better than you. To learn academics, hang out with learned men. To be a great mechanic, hang out with great mechanics.

To be daring, hang out with daring men.

Without the natural talents of some, nor the intellect of others, hanging out with daring men has been the singular road to any success I've achieved in life. The way I get there is by knowing people who will help me get there. I meet them by being the guy who always shows up.

My pastor, Phil Pringle, said it this way in his book *You, the Leader:* "The making of a man of God is a mixture of triumph and failure, blessing and pain. It takes much longer than anticipated, costs more than we want and takes us on a journey through far more trouble than we ever thought we could manage."[14]

God entrusts His kingdom to those He has tested and brought through the fire.

God builds daring men, to build a daring church.

Daring Men Are Faithful

My friend Al was in a difficult situation. He'd committed to be faithful to his leader. But the leader was in serious personal dysfunction, and the pressure on Al was intense. He could leave and walk away, and people would say, "Well, you had no other choice." But Al had made a promise. He wanted to walk out his word to the best of his ability, at least as long as it did not violate his own faith.

The Bible teaches us, "Be faithful in that which is another man's and God will give you your own" (Luke 16:12, my paraphrase). We're all willing to be faithful in favorable conditions, but nothing was going right here. Personal difficulties dogged leadership, and other managers in the national religious organization where he served were leaving, but Al was true to his word.

When God gives His word, He keeps His word. Keeping His word is why we trust His name. When we pray, we call on the name of God. The reason we can use His name with total faith is that His Word is always good.

A man's name is only as good as his word. Al kept his word, he held his tongue, and God gave him his destiny.

It was not easy. Many advised him to cut and run, but he stayed, confronting negative talk with a generous spirit of honor and grace. Then came the day he felt the release of God's Spirit through a tug on his heart. Then he was honest, told the leader how he felt, and God prospered him.

Today as the pastor of a thriving megachurch, Al and his family still enjoy the blessings of that faithfulness. He was faithful in that which was "another man's," and God gave him that which was his own. Even today, many years after his test of character, the words he expresses toward that leader are words of grace and wholeness. Al has inspired many, and I am one.

Faithfulness is the cornerstone of a godly character. Character is what sustains you through the tough times of life. It illuminates truth and brings right decisions.

**Character is the foundation of daring.
Without character, daring is just a blast of hot wind.**

Daring men of enduring character stay connected. Daring men are strong men by virtue of their godly character. *Strong men make strong families, and strong families make strong churches, and strong churches will transform culture.*

Daring men produce
transformation!

Joshua Grips the Promise

Joshua surveys the fortified Hebron strongholds from a rugged mountain close by Gilgal in Canaan. Standing with him is Caleb, his closest friend, fellow warrior, and the other spy who had the truth. They have faithfully followed Moses, won battles, crushed Jericho, grasped tightly the fight of faith, and endured the pain of perseverance. They are five years into occupying the Promised Land. It's been a grueling fight, but they stand energized by the view of the next pagan kingdom they are about to defeat.

Caleb turns to Joshua in a moment of reflection that goes something like this:

"Remember when you and I came back from this place? We stood right here and saw the place of freedom for our nation and a secure home for our families. We went back, and the negative attitudes of men who feared the enemy kept us from getting in."

Joshua turns, "I remember you telling all the people to quiet down, including Moses!"

"That was a stretch, I wasn't sure how he'd take that."

"Caleb, you had the word of truth. 'We are able to take this land! Don't worry about the enemy. Our God will defeat them all!'"

"Joshua, I couldn't back off. I was telling them what I saw in my heart. It was put there by God. The other spies were recounting what their own strength could do. And by that measure, we couldn't have defeated a small village of wimps! But I could 'see' it, I could see what God would do."

"Brother, we have defeated huge armies. We're building powerful cities. New farms are growing crops.

It's an intoxicating day of liberty! But, you and I know, none of this happens without the hand of Almighty God—no answer other than that. It certainly wasn't my great strategies."

"You're too humble. You do have the heart of a warrior, and we've taken the land. It's all been worth it. Every moment."

"Yeah, so let's go. We have to defeat those giants over there. If that's the mountain you want, *let's go get it!*"

Daring men "see" with their hearts.

What is desired in the natural must be first obtained in the supernatural.

Daring Men Fight for Their Destiny

Paul at the end of his life wrote, "I have fought the good fight, I have finished the race, I have kept the faith" (2 Timothy 4:7).

Trust God and His plans, not what we see, what He sees. *God knows!*

Without faith, it is impossible to please God.

Faith is the lifeblood of the kingdom.

Fear is the enemy of faith. It crushes the truth, defies God, and destroys your dreams.

Fear is what thwarted Joshua and Caleb the first time they arrived at the nation promised to them by God—the land of Canaan.

Stories of the Old Testament are pictures for us to discern and learn from. In this one, Israel was about to enter its destiny, the Promised Land, the place where God designed for them to live in total fulfillment of all they were to be on the earth. The Promised Land is a picture of how we are to live—in a land of promise, completing our destiny.

All twelve spies brought back the same technical report, but spiritually they were 180 degrees apart. Two men, Joshua and Caleb said, "It's a great place, full of struggles and fights, but our God can take it for us."

The spirit of fear in the ten other spies told them they were small, like grasshoppers in the sight of the issues facing them—fortified cities, giants, and hardships. Because people are negative by nature, fear gripped the hearts of the people. They rejected the faith of Joshua and Caleb and turned away. When they realized their sin, some tried to take the land only to be routed in a massacre. So they wandered in the deserts of the Middle

East for forty years. Only two of the people who had stood on the threshold of their destiny ever entered in. The rest died because of fear. Only two of that generation entered Canaan—Joshua and Caleb.

Caleb had trusted God to win the victories.

Caleb said to his friend Joshua, "I brought back a report as it was in my heart" (Joshua 14:7). Caleb's heart trusted God. Caleb believed in a big God! It was in his heart, so the struggles and armies of the enemy did not look larger than God. Caleb had perspective: BIG GOD, small devil.

We learn five keys from Joshua and Caleb's faith in God that apply to our lives today.

First, you have an unlimited source of strength.

God is so big that when He gives away power, He loses no power. When He uses His power, He is not diminished. And He is for you, not against you.

My wife's favorite section of Scripture is one written on my heart as well. Here it is in the Amplified version:

> *"For He [God] Himself has said, I will not in any way fail you nor give you up nor leave you without support. [I will] not, [I will] not, [I will] not in any degree leave you helpless nor forsake nor let [you] down (relax My hold on you)! [Assuredly not!]*
>
> *So we take comfort and are encouraged and **confidently and boldly say**, The Lord is my Helper; I will not be seized with alarm [I*

*will not fear or dread or be terrified]. What
can man do to me?"*

(Hebrews 13:5–6, AMP)

Like Caleb, let that be the center of your heart.
You have the strength of the name of Jesus. You are a
powerful force by the strong arm of Almighty God!

Second, it is your land.

Even when you have not yet taken a step on it, it is
yours. Your destiny does not belong to anyone else. It is
yours, but you must take it.

*God has never put your destiny in the hands of your
enemy. And He never will.*

Jesus said, "What I have been given, I give to you."

He gave us the power to be heirs with Him, along
with all the rights to be children of God. Not just
servants, though we serve. Not just workers, though we
work. Not just friends, though we have a relationship of
friends. BUT, CHILDREN.

That means we have ACCESS! The barriers of the old
covenant have been removed, the formalized methods
of the courts have been removed, and now, like kids at
home—we have access to our Father in heaven. And, He
said, "Whatever you need, ask me."

Jesus on the cross of Calvary took title to the destiny
of mankind and the earth—the world will be His
kingdom, His gift from the Father—and we will see the
world become a better place.

It is your land—your destiny.

Third, don't look back.

Proverbs says the way of the righteous winds ever upward. Paul said the call of God is an upward call. Living in the past, looking back at past failures, and looking back at past temptations or decisions not done exactly right will make you a prisoner of history.

The true ministry of the Gospel is not about pushing information down into people, but pulling people up into God's VISION for their lives.

It's the direction of your focus.

Religion keeps us looking back. Following Christ is about looking forward and being a creator of a new future rather than a victim of our past history.

Looking back will cause us to make decisions based on our failures rather than on the vision of the future. We learn from the past, *but we don't live in it!* I had a friend who talked about past times—great days in high school and fun times in college. Now, in his later years, he has never succeeded in focusing on what his life is to become. And, it's almost over!

> *God is feeding us the timeline of our lives*
>   *from the future.*
> *We're living it from our past.*
> *Where the two meet is called "today."*
> *God delivers us TO righteousness,*
>   *by delivering us FROM sin.*
> *God is more focused on where we're going*
>   *than on where we've been.*

Look forward. And keep moving. The baseball Hall-of-Famer Satchel Paige, who pitched until he was sixty years old, once said: "Don't look back. Something might be gaining on you!"[17]

Funny and myopic, but nonetheless when you focus on your destiny, the battles of today will have a purpose. It's in your purpose that you'll find your strength.

Fourth, never quit.

Failure is never fatal, quitting is. Most people quit just before the leading edge of victory.

> *"But anyone who is right with me thrives on loyal trust; if he cuts and runs, I won't be very happy. But we're not quitters who lose out. Oh, no! We'll stay with it and survive, trusting all the way"* *(Hebrews 10:38–39, THE MESSAGE).*

Stories of those who never quit are the heroic stories that lift our hearts. The key to success in life is not quitting. Don't give up.

It is said that the majority of success in our lives comes from just showing up.

> "Champions are not those who never fail. They are those who never quit. *God never quits on you, so we don't quit on God—or ourselves."* Ed Cole

Fifth, BIG GOD/small devil!

Simple, yet profound concept. Caleb captured it, and it changed his life. It got him from the wilderness to

Canaan and paved the way for his future, his family's future, and their families' futures.

It's just this: *God is bigger.* He is bigger than any giant. God put the giant there only to make Caleb bigger—bigger than any unpaid payroll, bigger than the crush of betrayal or any emotion, bigger than every failure, and bigger than every temptation to sin—BIGGER.

> *"And Jesus came and spoke to them, saying, 'All authority has been given to Me in heaven and on earth. Go therefore and make disciples of all the nations, baptizing them in the name of the Father and of the Son and of the Holy Spirit, teaching them to observe all things that I have commanded you; and* lo, I am with you always, even to the end of the age'" *(Matthew 28:18–20, NKJV, emphasis added).*

The Bible is filled with promises that He will be there for us. It says: "You will make it." "You will be an overcomer."

Will you be hurt by persecution? Yes! Can it destroy you? No!

Paul said, "If I die, I win. If I live, I win" (Philippians 1:21, my paraphrase).

BIGGER!

Nothing in this world can take the place of persistence. Talent will not; nothing is more common than unsuccessful men with great talent. Genius will not; unrewarded genius is almost a proverb. Education will not; the world is full of educated derelicts. Persistence, determination alone are omnipotent.[16]

- Calvin Coolidge, U.S. President

DARING MEN TRAIN TO WIN

4

My Father's Beard

I love this photo of my dad.

He's laughing, and I love that memory of him. But in this photo, he has a beard. That was very rare. The beard is what actually means something. It's meaningful in two ways.

First, he grew it while we were on a weeklong horseback camping trip with Ron and Burke in the high Sierra Nevada mountain range of Northern California. It was an awesome trip. It was a rare dad-son time for us. It meant the world to me as a young teenager trying to grow into a man. The beard is special. It's my special memory. My dad as a rugged man. My dad as my dad. Mine.

Secondly, the photo was taken at a dinner meeting a few days after our camping trip. Dad had flown to a special meeting at his denomination's headquarters. He decided to keep the beard. The father in him wanted to relish the memory of the time he took his son on a horseback camping trip. Now, he was at a banquet where he would accept the position to lead a major part of that group, a new thrust to train young men. In his mind, the beard was fitting. But the beard was not acceptable. Beards were out of style with those men, and Dad knew it. He thought they could accept him for who they knew him to be. To him, it was about character, principle, and truth. To them, he was politically incorrect.

In a surprise announcement, the position was given to another man. Everyone applauded, shook hands, and dad flew home.

The world is a better place for him not getting the position.

And, I was a healthier boy with great memories as a man.

And now it can be your memory, too.

This is what a dad does.

And the things you have heard from me among many witnesses, commit these words to faithful men who will be able to teach others also (2 Timothy 2:2, NKJV).

The apostle Paul is training his protégé Timothy, a young leader who had been raised by a mother and grandmother. Paul was teaching him the core of character—faithfulness. Paul tells him to find faithful men, not just talented or charismatic, but faithful men.

Paul wrote Timothy two major letters that became part of the Bible, teaching him biblical manhood and leadership. In this passage of Scripture is the description of four generations—God committing to righteous legacy, transferring the lessons from one age, and teaching the next age to teach the new one coming up, so that each generation can teach the next. This is what a spiritual dad does.

The world looks for talent,
God commits to character.
While the world looks for
better methods, God looks for
better men.[18]

~ *E. M. Bounds*

Talent can take you
where your character cannot
sustain you.[19]

~ *Edwin Louis Cole*

Toward Daring Manhood

With the landmark book, *Maximized Manhood*, published in 1982 and written by my dad, men all over the world tried to gain a foothold on a fragmented landscape that had been violently shaken by a distorted image of manhood and masculinity.

Under Dad's mentoring, hundreds of thousands of men successfully reversed their course from watered-down masculinity toward being solid, real men. In a world with billions of men, this fresh wave of "real manhood" worked, but it must be reproduced and reproduced again. That's where you and I step in.

We can no longer depend on leaders from the past or insipid pancake breakfast progams. We have to do it ourselves. We have to have the daring guts within ourselves to face life like a man. If we don't, then we have only ourselves to blame for the state of the world, the condition of our families, and the quality of our own lifestyle. It's up to us.

It's an internal battle. But external attacks are relentless and focused on tearing down your determination to be a real man. The media's general portrayals of men as weak, insipid fathers, and worthless husbands dull the senses. Then the real-life correlation we read in the news media about corruption in leadership, scandalous politicians, and evil predators all serve to weaken the image we hold of ourselves as men.

Caught up in what we see, we second-guess our masculinity, wallow in the compromised images of manhood, or perhaps just give it all up, crack open a beer, and sit in front of a television or game station hoping no one will require our attention.

The truth is, you're in your own personal war. You know what's at stake.

A new book claims to shed light on the historic tragedy of the sinking of the luxury liner, the *Titanic*.[20] The claim is that the steersman, in the panic to avoid an iceberg, forgot that the new ships' steering mechanism required one to turn the wheel in the opposite direction of how the old ships steered. The man steered the ship right into the iceberg that purportedly sank it.

But that still wasn't what sank the ship. The official with the company that owned the ship ordered that they continue steaming forward. Had they stopped, there would have been time for the rescue ship to come. Most of the lives would have been saved that perished in the icy seas that night.

It's your life, and you're the captain of it.

You are personally accountable for your failures—to admit them, get the help you need, course correct, and move on beyond what is past. You are liable for your own life and for the stewardship of whatever family or relationships you find yourself in. You alone are responsible for the gifts, talents, and abilities God has given you.

Most men need help forming a plan. That's why today, thousands of churches worldwide use our Majoring in Men Curriculum.

And then we need the daring—the guts—to follow it!

Character. Daring. Guts.
A man you can depend on.
The man you want beside
you in a fight.

Spiritual Health Daily Workout

For a positive workout physically, you have to work the core. That center of your body will hold everything else together in health and strength. In the same way, we need 'centering' in our spiritual lives, a workout that develops a strong core.

Here's a start to building a strong core, a good spiritual workout. This is a strategic plan that will build faith and defeat fear. It will instill new levels of daring into your heart. This is practical, and you can do it. So, start.

• TURN OFF: TV, radio, news, sports radio, and talk shows. Don't dwell on negative media images and words. If it's your job and you need to know, then control the times. When you're not working or you've learned what you need to know, turn it off. Don't just keep your mind open to the stress, restlessness, and rebellion of the culture.

• TURN ON: Messages of faith, peace, and uplifting power. Start with the messages of your own pastor and leaders you know. I've written some in the back of the book that encourage me.

"So then faith comes by hearing, and hearing by the word of God" (Romans 10:17).

• READ Proverbs every morning. Read Psalms every evening.

This will give you wisdom for the day and get courage working in your heart and soul in the evening. It will help you rest, and refresh you as you sleep.

• ENCOURAGE others! Speak life into those around you.

Be connected to men around you. Go out of your way to say something positive. If that is unusual where you live, then others may laugh at you. But your own heart will believe the sound of your voice, and your spirit will soar.

• PRAY - For yourself, for others you know, for those in authority, for your brothers and sisters around the world going through great trials.

Prayer produces intimacy with God, with those you pray with, and with those for whom you are praying. Prayer centers the heart.

• DECLARE faith over your life!

Words have creative power. Pray God's Word over yourself.

Start with Psalm 37. Read it aloud, over you, your family, your business. How? Just insert your name, the names of your family members, as you read it like a prayer to the Lord. He is faithful to perform His Word.

• MEDITATE on the Word of God. That means think about it on purpose and with deep intent. Find one verse of Scripture each morning to think about deeply. During the day, trigger your mind to think about the good things God has done in your life.

Write in a journal words of life, peace, questions, prayers, and answers—keep it nearby to encourage yourself when you need it.

• ATTEND connect groups, and SHOW UP at church meetings.

• LISTEN to godly music in the car and at home. You set the atmosphere of your home just by the music you play. When you're going through a tough time, put on earphones and listen to Scripture or to select songs of praise that soothe your soul and boost your spirit.

- DO the smart, wise things in your job, career, school, family, and friendships.

Live life with margin, keeping a little change in your pocket. Be early for meetings. Help meet the needs of others.

- DECREASE debt as fast as possible and never get into debt again. Streamline and simplify your life. Learn the level of your capacity.

- TITHE regularly. This is God's system for financial health that works so well, even secular experts advise it. Get into God's system of finance by getting out of the cultural norms of success, money, life, and things.

Why don't you tell yourself out loud right now, "I need to do this and I need to start today."

"Time lost is time lost. It's gone forever. Some people tell themselves that they will work twice as hard tomorrow to make up for what they did not do today. People should always do their best. If they work twice as hard tomorrow, then they should have also worked twice as hard today. That would have been their best."

~ Coach John Wooden
Legendary UCLA Coach
Ten Time National Champion

Daring Direction

We all want the basic feeling of security. We don't want bombs dropping on us, guys jacking our car or the fear of being hit by stray bullets as we walk out of our bedroom in the morning. If we're fortunate to live where those things don't normally occur, we're on the path to feeling secure.

We want financial security as well, the ability to make a living and perhaps a little more. We enjoy the feeling of being able to buy shoes for our kids, take our wives or girlfriends out for dinner, get our car fixed when it breaks, or help a buddy through a tough time. We intensely dislike the feeling of not being able to afford the basics—shelter, food, and clothing. If we're fortunate to have steady work, we're even further up the path toward feelings of security and safety.

But security can be a trap, and safety an illusion. The homogenized mall environments, going the same way to work, TV shows we watch on Tuesdays, guys we play cards with on Fridays, and the lowered expectations of culture can all numbingly rock us to sleep in our manhood. Without a visible enemy, pangs of hunger, or a reason to run, we just sit flipping channels and surfing the web, waiting for something to grab our attention. To medicate the pressures of stress and turmoil, we immerse ourselves in toys, hobbies, habits, trivial pursuits, fishing poles, bar stools and La-Z-Boy chairs as life seeps casually out the door. Is this really the way we want to live? To leave earth without even a whimper of fight in us?

It's time to jettison complacent security as a goal, much less a way of life.

It's time we ourselves become dangerous and daring, not just watch someone else!

Daring men look into what politicians are doing and let their voice be heard. Daring men click off the television. Daring men report a drunk driver. Daring men go to their children's parent-teacher meetings at school. Daring men are connected to church, support their pastor, and clean the restrooms. Daring men make themselves available. Daring men face reality. Daring men... You can fill in the list. You have a sense of what it is to be a daring man even if you're not doing it. We all know you want to!

Daring men are not satisfied with status quo. Daring men are willing to be different.

Let's set some basic guidelines as we push further into the daring life:

You're not your dad.

Whether your dad helped launch cultural transformation, or whether he was an absentee, addict, abuser, or adulterer, it's time to move on. You may say, "My dad was the greatest...(fill in the blank)." "My dad and I used to..." "My dad never..." It's time to let go of any expectations or disappointments. The pressure you put on yourself to be like your dad or never to be like your dad is bogus.

You're not your dad.

If he was a bad guy, the way you move on is by forgiving him, even if he's dead or won't listen. Have a conversation with him out in the woods when he's not even there. Write him a letter that you never send. Do whatever it takes, but get past it. If he was a good guy, follow his example in what he did right and use it as a springboard to get on with your own personal shape of manhood.

Once you let go, you're free to be a genuine, original, daring man of God.

You need a plan.

No millionaire who sustained his riches ever got there by accident. Plenty of people have accidentally won or found millions, but most don't keep it unless they create a plan. What is easy to obtain is difficult to maintain, and that is true of money, cars, and sometimes marriage.

In the same way you win a lotto ticket, you may get a wife, have some kids, or find a job, but you'll never sustain them, much less help them become the best they can be, unless you have a plan. This book has the building blocks, but its up to you to be the construction chief. Get your plan together, then do it. Grab the men's curriculum and make it happen!

Your honor defines you.

Honor is that intangible we notice most often only when it's missing. A man is commanded to love his wife, but the Bible says for a woman to "honor" her husband.

Honor is valuing others as highly as yourself. Honor is based on integrity, worked out in grace, and shown by respect. Honor lifts others up into their destiny.

Dishonor brings dysfunction.

One of the leading causes of divorce is the loss of respect between spouses. This is true also of business partners, friendships, and even church members' relationships with their pastors. Men today must learn to show respect to others, and learn to respect themselves as well. Tolerance will never transform a country or your company, but honor and mutual respect will.

Honoring others and being concerned about others shows respect. And, hey, respect yourself enough to stay fit, invest time in your spiritual life, and don't give your word unless you expect to keep it. There's more, but that gets us started in a new direction.

Right

    About

        Now...

            is when you'll have to start thinking about accepting responsibility for what you're reading.

Or, you can just throw the book away. But tossing it out won't change where you need to go.

Whatever it takes to motivate you toward becoming the kind of daring man we're talking about, do that thing.

Put yourself in the crosshairs of a bold lifestyle. It may get uncomfortable, or seem challenging. But if you're willing to grip the grace, you'll be headed in the right direction.

Righteous men of daring spirit are not always popular in culture. But they are the only kind of men God chooses.

Character is the foundation of
success. Faithfulness is
the bedrock of character.
Faithfulness is proved in obedience.
Obedience is a mark of maturity.

Maturity is doing the
right thing, when it needs to
be done, regardless of the
circumstances, emotions or
temptations of the moment.

DARING MEN FACE THEIR FEARS

Daring Men Face FEAR

Joshua has won some battles. The nation has crossed a huge mind-obstacle by crossing the Jordan and going into Canaan, their promised land. But they're still carrying many of the doubts created by centuries of slavery, years of wandering, and fears about their abilities.

Now, they've come up against Jericho. It's not an unknown. Their fathers traveled by there for generations. It's a well-known, powerful, strong, and wealthy city. And, that's the real issue. They know how strong it is.

Jericho is a fortress with walls twenty feet thick, soaring seventy-five feet high, and had never been conquered in over two thousand years. It was a place so powerful that the local people used it as a source of strength when they prayed to their gods, to "the god of Jericho" that could never be defeated. It was a place of refuge to those in it and a source of pride to all who were around it.

Joshua *could* lead the people by Jericho, head to the plains in the north, the mountains to the east, fight some easier battles, get settled into the land, and then come back to try to defeat Jericho.

But God wanted them to face their largest fear.

It was in that place that God wanted to prove His strength compared to their strength, to show Himself strong once the people knew their own weakness.

Fear arrives uninvited. Our choice is to open or close the door. Fear easily fills our thoughts. Negative words, thoughts, and emotions will cause fear to overtake our lives.

Daring men face fear.

The defeat of fear is the embrace of faith.

Paul said at the end of his life, "I have fought the good fight, I have finished the race, I have kept the faith" (2 Timothy 4:7).

Keeping the faith. That is the lifeblood of the kingdom of God. The Bible teaches that without faith, it's impossible to walk out God's path.

Faith is believing God will do what He said He would do.

Faith is an action. Faith is an aggressive stance.

If you have faith, but don't do anything, then where's the proof that you have it?

Faith is not what you passively *have*.

Faith is what you aggressively *do*.

God will take you to the place of your greatest fears, so you will not be defeated by fear.

My dad taught us:

Faith is believing what you cannot see will come to pass.

Fear is believing what you cannot see will come to pass.

Same definition, different sources, and far different results.

Trusting God is committing to His words and ways. In the face of the facts, trust the truth, Jesus Himself.

Fear is a natural human emotion. When used for its proper purpose, fear keeps us from getting swept away by the waves, burning our legs on the exhaust pipe, or cutting ourselves with the saw. But in our spiritual lives, fear becomes a trap.

Holding onto fear is a natural human condition. We are negative by nature. So overcoming fear must come from a "super-natural" source—one that is not subject to natural results.

The embrace of faith is the defeat of fear. You can try defeating it by thinking better thoughts, or looking in the mirror and chanting "You're the man!" before you leave the house. But later that same day, negativity still overtakes us. Sure, we're "the man," only now we're the man who is in full fear mode!

Courage is the virtue of leadership.

"Never give in. Never give in. Never, never, never, never—in nothing, great or small, large or petty—never give in, except to convictions of honor and good sense.

Never yield to force.

Never yield to the apparently overwhelming might of the enemy."[21]

~ Winston Churchill
Harrow School, 1941, Excerpt from a speech during the air bombardment of London

Daring Men Speak Faith

There is a great story in the New Testament Gospel of St. Luke. The disciples, Jesus' closest friends, are with Him in a boat on a huge lake in Israel.

Winds unexpectedly sweep down from the mountains on the eastern edge. A violent storm erupts, a storm so intense they actually fear they could die. These are the disciples, Jesus' best friends. They are with Jesus. They have Him in the boat—and yet—*they are covered up with fear!*

It is natural to have fear. But Jesus stopped the storm. Jesus declared faith against fear, and peace against the storm (Luke 8). Peace is defined by the world as "the absence of war," but God says true peace is *His presence in the middle of a war.* He is the peace in the storm!

"Don't keep on worrying about anything, but in everything pray! Then God's peace will guard you like a sentinel—your heart and mind secured" (Philippians 4:6).

Jesus told the disciples that fear overwhelmed them because their faith was not strong. It was a violent storm. It was a real danger. Fear was a natural emotion. But their response to the emotion was way off.

Worry is a substitute for prayer. Don't worry. Pray.

Our response must be to do what Jesus did and act in faith. Any one of Jesus' disciples could have spoken faith into fear and peace into the storm and stopped it. And after what they saw that night, they all learned.

> *God did not give us a spirit of timidity (of cowardice, of craven and cringing and fawning fear), but [He has given us a spirit] of power and of love and of calm and well-balanced mind and discipline and self-control (2 Timothy 1:7, AMP).*

In the Book of Romans, we read that God has set the entire world within a system that leads to frustration. The Law cannot be fully followed, and human nature, outside of God's Spirit, cannot please God. So we're frustrated on many levels. Nothing we do feels that it's good enough nor fully satisfies us (Romans 8:1–17). The earthly system God set up is one predestined for failure because that very weakness brings men to Christ. In Him, the Law is fully satisfied through His grace, and our deepest fulfillment is found by living according to the leading of His Spirit.

Operating by the world system of thought will always result in frustration and makes men prone to become slaves to fear. But when we are liberated from that bondage and made a child of the life-giving God, we have the power of Christ to fight every fear.

Here is God's promise for you as a follower of Christ:

> *Jesus answered them, ... "The Father is with me. I've told you all this so that **trusting me, you will be unshakable** and assured, deeply at peace. In this godless world you will continue to experience difficulties. But take heart! I've conquered the world" (John 16:31–33, THE MESSAGE, emphasis added).*

For the followers of Christ, the finish is always positive, whether here on earth or on the other side with Christ. Negative situations will not last.

God finishes what He begins.

What God does always ends on a positive.

> *I thank my God upon every remembrance of you, always in every prayer of mine making request for you all with joy, for your fellowship in the gospel from the first day until now, being* **confident** *of this very thing, that He who has begun a good work in you will complete it until the day of Jesus Christ.*
> *~ Philippians 1:3–6, NKJV, emphasis added*

Optimism vs. Faith

Vice Admiral James Stockdale was leading air attacks in his A-4E Skyhawk when he was shot down over enemy territory on September 9, 1965.[22] He was the highest ranking officer ever captured by the North Vietnamese armies. He endured terrible atrocities and hardships through eight excruciating years in captivity.

How he made it mentally through the beatings, torture, and being crammed into a 3' x 9' cell with lights on twenty-four hours a day has become known as the "Stockdale Paradox."

Stockdale was asked if "being an optimist" helped him get through the numbing pain. Stockdale replied, "I never lost faith in the end of the story. I never doubted not only that I would get out, but also that I would prevail in the end and turn the experience into the defining event of my life, which, in retrospect, I would not trade....The ones who didn't make it out were the optimists....They were the ones who said, 'We're going to be out by Christmas.' And Christmas would come, and Christmas would go. Then they'd say, 'We're going to be out by Easter.' And Easter would come, and Easter would go. And then Thanksgiving, and then it would be Christmas again. And they died of a broken heart."

Stockdale then added:

"This is a very important lesson. You must never confuse faith that you will prevail in the end—which you can never afford to lose—with the discipline to confront the most brutal facts of your current reality, whatever they might be."

We do not base our life on emotional optimism, but on the solid truth of God's Word, which has never failed, will never fail, and cannot fail. Reading the Word regularly will produce a feeling of total confidence in Him. That confidence becomes the energy to discipline our lives to endurance.

The daring endurance of the Christian life is based on faith, not optimism.

Enthusiasm is a motivating force, but you cannot build your life on it.

Optimism is an attitude that keeps a person positive in outlook but is unable to sustain life through storms.

Faith is a substance! Faith is that substance upon which life can be built with truth at its foundation.

Faith faces reality. It is not blind. Faith produces clear vision.

Faith is a foundational substance, which produces a feeling of confidence that God will do what He said He would do!

> *Happy are those who don't listen to the wicked, who don't go where sinners go, who don't do what evil people do. They love the Lord's teachings, and they think about those teachings day and night. **They are strong**, like a tree planted by a river. The tree produces fruit in season, and its leaves don't die. Everything they do will succeed.*
> ~ *Psalm 1:1–3,* NCV

Both faith and fear have properties of attraction.

Faith attracts the positive
Fear attracts the negative

If you don't believe in the law of gravity, it still exists and it still works. If you don't believe in the laws of faith or fear, they still work.

"Fear not, for I am with you. Be not dismayed; for I am your God. I will strengthen you. Yes, I will help you, I will uphold you with my righteous right hand" (Isaiah 41:10, NKJV).

"May the God of hope fill you with all joy and peace as you trust in him, so that you may overflow with hope by the power of the Holy Spirit" (Romans 15:13, NIV).

DARING MEN ENDURE

Daring Men Have Endurance

Your circumstances do not dictate God's response to faith!

God always has a strategy. Jesus always had an answer in every situation! Trusting God fuels endurance and your endurance qualifies you for promotion.

In the New Testament Book of Hebrews, Paul writes:

"Patient endurance is what you need now, so that you will continue to do God's will. Then you will receive all that He has promised. For in just a little while, the Coming One will come and not delay. And my righteous ones will live by faith. But I will take no pleasure in anyone who turns away" (Hebrews 10:36, NLT).

Another Bible translation puts it this way: *"But you need to stick it out [endure], staying with God's plan so you'll be there for the promised completion. It won't be long now, He's on the way; He'll show up most any minute"* (THE MESSAGE).

Then Paul sounds a triumphant call to daring men: *"But we are not like those who turn away from God to their own destruction. We are the faithful ones, whose souls will be saved"* (v. 39). Endurance is not just hanging out until God does something. Endurance is an active, unstoppable, and fearless move toward the desired result. Endurance moves, pushes, struggles, and pulls until only the power of God can finish.

Endurance is not the denial of obstacles but crawling over them with bloodied knuckles.

Kurt Warner's story is the picture of an enduring warrior. He is former all-pro American football player. Kurt came out of a small high school and went to a local college in Iowa. He was the third-string quarterback until he finally got to play his last year in college and did well that year. Out of college, none of the professional teams wanted him as a player, so he spent the next few months stocking shelves in a grocery store and helping coach at the college he'd attended.

Still trying to be a professional football player, he applied to any type of team he could find, finally getting a job at the marginal, minor league indoor arena football league. He excelled there for two years. Yet still, the only offer he received was to play in the European National Football Leagues.

He never quit working toward his dream.

Kurt did well in Europe and finally, five years after leaving college, he got a shot at playing for the Rams football team. There, and with other teams in the National Football League, Kurt became one of the greatest quarterbacks ever to play professional American football.

When asked how it all happened, Kurt explained how he kept faith in his dreams:

"I believe that the Lord has a plan for each of us that's better than anything we can imagine—even if that plan isn't obvious to us at every stage. He prepared me for this over a long period of time—in lower-profile locker rooms and the grocery store and in Europe, through all the personal tragedies and in spite of the people who doubted me along the way."[23]

The New Testament was written and translated primarily in the Greek language. The definitions of *endurance* in the Greek are very uplifting. The word *hupomone* is most often used for *endurance*, which comes from the root word *hupomeno*. Here are the meanings:

> cheerful (or hopeful), constancy: patience to remain to undergo, bear (trials), persevere: abide, endure (take) patient suffer, tarry be-hind...*to spend a little more time*[24]

Success is the result of constancy of purpose.

Most people who are successful in life have faced obstacles. Nothing worthwhile comes without great effort. It is in the will that endurance is found.

The will to win is not as important as the will to prepare to win. The legendary coach John Wooden said, "Failure to prepare is preparation for failure."[25] Endurance is preparing for the win, when you're not even sure you're getting into the game.

It is said that the daring explorer Ernest Shackleton once put an ad in the London newspapers that stated: "Men wanted for hazardous journey. Low wages, bitter cold, long hours of complete darkness. Safe return doubtful. Honour and recognition in event of success."[26]

Shackleton's most famous exploration was the attempted crossing of Antarctica in 1915. Equipping a boat and a crew of fifty-four men, they survived massive waves and crushing seas but arrived late in the season, which trapped them in polar ice floes. As the crushing ice strangled the ship, they abandoned it as it sunk and floated on an iceberg for days. Then, finally crawling on broken ice over the churning seas, they found an island. After 497 days of being on the water, they were not rescued. Shackleton and five others sailed a small boat into massive hurricanes, climbed the back of a rugged mountain of ice and thirty days later, after a final thirty-six straight hours of arduous climbing, they found safety. They took ships back for the rest of the crew and did not lose a man.

The name of his ship was *The Endurance*.

Shackleton never achieved the goals of being the first to the South Pole or of crossing Antarctica on foot. The first to reach the South Pole is a Norwegian named Roald Amundsen. The first to cross Antarctica by way of the South Pole was Sir Edmund Hillary but his fame in being the first to conquer Mount Everest eclipsed it. Instead, the most fame for an arctic explorer went to a man of uncommon daring and endurance, whose only record was that he attempted something bigger than himself—Shackleton.

Most men, in the brooding darkness of the deep of night, quit just before the brilliant dawning of the victorious day. But daring men have the kind of endurance that is willing to do whatever it takes to have even the slightest glimpse of the promised goal.

Daring Men Have Focus

The power of the life of Jesus as a man apart from His divinity was the clear, undistracted focus of his life. Jesus never wasted a moment, a thought, a day, nor was He ever distracted from His purpose.

Jesus had a goal. His goal directed His thinking, decision-making, preparation, timing, and priorities.

Joshua had a goal also: Defeat the enemy and get the nation into the Promised Land. Having a clear goal, or focus, gave Joshua clarity of thought. Having direction, a goal and a purpose gave Him courage, energy and endurance.

The ancient Chinese war strategist Sun Tzu taught:

"One who is confused in his purpose cannot respond to his enemy."[27]

We all need a target to go after. That's what gives us focus, purpose, ability to make decisions, energy, and the ability to risk. The old adage is, "If you don't know where you're going, any road will take you there."

Marcus Aurelius said:

"The true worth of a man is to be measured by the objects he pursues."[28]

Nolan Ryan was a great baseball player. He was a pitcher, the one who throws the ball to the batter. That was his main job, so he totally focused on throwing the ball. What made him one of the greatest who ever played was his consistent focus on the goal. He had a target, and he was able to hit it over and over again. For years. From 60 feet at 95 miles per hour.

Many others have thrown as many times without tiring. Many can throw as fast. But very few ever stayed as consistently focused on the target.

On occasion, I work out at a gym. There are always dozens of men training at various stages of effort and ability. I don't train so I can wear tight shirts. I train to be healthy and to keep my heart in shape, so I get that much done.

But, if you told me that next week I was fighting the boxing champion of the world—NOW I'm motivated in my workout. I would be focused, and I'd work harder than ever, because I don't want to die!

Most people live life without a clear target.

So they listen to the last voice they've heard.

The principle is:

Whatever captures and holds your attention, will eventually control the direction of your life.

The Bible recounts the story of Job, a man who lost his dreams. His family was dead, wiped out. His money was gone. His life had collapsed, and he lost his focus. He said: "I do not have the strength to endure" (Job 6:11). Job was saying, *"I do not have a goal that encourages me to carry on."*

"Do I have the strength of a stone? Is my body made of bronze? No, I am utterly helpless, without any chance of success" (Job 6:12–13, NLT).

What finally rescued this man from his fear and despair was his renewed focus on God as his source of life. Focus renewed his strength.

We need targets in life or we'll feel helpless, drifting, without chance of success. Columbus sailed from Spain to America in difficult circumstances, drenched with doubt from those around him, and the fears from every wise man in Europe. What sustained Columbus while sailing on the open seas, with no sight of land from August 3 to October 11 was that he had a target. In his journal, he wrote repeatedly, "Continued west."[29]

Paul the apostle wrote, "Remember that in a race, everyone runs, but only one person gets the prize. You also must run in such a way that you will win. All athletes practice strict self-control. They do it to win a prize that will fade away, but we do it for an eternal prize. *So I run straight to the goal* with purpose in every step. I am not like a boxer who misses his punches. I discipline my body like an athlete, training it to do what it should. Otherwise, I fear that after preaching to others I myself might be disqualified" (1 Corinthians 9:24–27, emphasis added).

Focus on the right target, then
RUN TO WIN, NOT JUST TO RUN!

"They look everywhere except to heaven, to the Most High. They are like a crooked bow that always misses its target" (Hosea 7:16, NLT).

The problem is aiming at the wrong target. Having our aim off.

"If you are aiming for nothing, you've already hit it."

My great-uncle, Dave Wharton, had a farm in what is now south Arlington, Texas. As a kid from California, going there in my early teens was a blast. We hunted gophers, shot guns, and rode bikes down dusty country roads.

Then one day, as I watched Uncle Dave traveling back and forth plowing a field, churning up the rich brown soil with his tractor, he motioned to me. "Get up on the tractor with me," he said.

I scrambled up the rig. He put me on his knees and told me to grab the steering wheel of the rumbling John Deere. I did not want to mess up, so I intently watched the front tires as he gunned the engine and the tractor lurched back through the field. Dirt clods jerked the wheel in my hands. I held on tight, focused on the tires, plowing through the dirt.

As we approached the fence that marked the southern end of the field, I was pumped. I did it! Then, we both turned and looked back. Oh no. It looked like the result of a drunken nightmare binge. I had just plowed a diagonal swath across Uncle's Dave's beautiful field.

He smiled. "OK, now we'll do it a little differently. We'll turn around and, you see that telephone pole down yonder? You just look at that, and keep pointing the tractor that direction. No matter what happens, don't look down. Look at the pole."

What a difference as I finished my second furrow! We looked back, and it was almost straight. I had stopped focusing on the little obstacles in front of the tires. I had lifted my eyes to the horizon, to the end of the field, and focused on the goal.

A friend of mine, Bruce, took a short course in driving at a local racetrack. He discovered something interesting. When they were training the drivers to race, the instructors would put them into a low-risk spin, turning the car in a circle on the track, telling the driver to get out of the spin.

Invariably, the young drivers would see where the car was going and try to avoid any obstacles, fighting like crazy to get back on the track. Then the instructor would tell them the secret: "When your car is in a spin, don't look where the car is going, look toward where you want it to go. The car will follow your focus."

Where you're focused is where you're eventually headed.

Chuck Colson was a fast-track climber in government circles. As a young man, he had the prestigious position of personal legal counsel to President Nixon.

His target was power. No matter what it took, what it cost, or who it hurt, Colson wanted to get power for his boss and for himself.

Out of the unethical results of that focus, Colson went to prison. During seven months in an Alabama jail, he was captured by the gospel of Jesus Christ. His life was changed, as was his target for life.

He found a new focus—to minister to people in prison wherever they were, however he could. A new focus, a new challenge. Out of that has come the largest prison ministry in the world, Prison Fellowship, with ministry to millions of prisoners and their families around the world.

Colson changed his target and it redirected his life.

What you're targeting—what you're focusing on—is where your life will go.

You may have a target, or you may be like most men, who are "targetless," not sure where they're supposed to be headed, and floating in and out of the winds of life.

There are basic targets for every man. Let's get clear focus, and let's bracket in the two most important targets.

Matthew wrote about the time Jesus was asked about targets. Religious leaders trying to trip Him up on technicalities asked Him, "Which is the most important commandment in the law of Moses?" (Matthew 22:36).

Jesus replied to them, "Let me give you two targets that everything else in life is based on. 'You must love the Lord your God with all your heart, with all your soul, and with all your mind.' This is the first and most important focus, and second but equally as important, 'Love the people around you with the same weight as what you love yourself'" (Matthew 22:37–40, my paraphrase).

There it is. When you focus on these two targets, your other targets will appear. If you have direction, dreams, or personal targets, but you've neglected these, you'll miss your target until you do this.

Jesus gave us the largest targets possible. Something we could hit. When we hit these big ones, the others get easier.

When my sons were young, we had a basketball hoop that could be lowered to their size. When it was low, they could make baskets. It built their confidence. As they grew, we took the basket higher each year until it was at the full height. Wanting the boys to be successful, I had made it in such a way they could compete even as young boys. Their confidence was strong, because they started with targets that were close enough to appear big to them.

Our Father in heaven wants us to be successful and to fulfill our design and purpose.

"Dear brothers and sisters, what's the use of saying you have faith if you don't prove it by your actions? (James 2:14).

"But if anyone has enough money to live well and sees a brother or sister in need and refuses to help—how can God's love be in that person?" (1 John 3:17).

"So now I am giving you a new commandment: Love each other. Just as I have loved you, you should love each other. Your love for one another will prove to the world that you are my disciples" (John 13:34–35, NLT).

"What this means is that those who become Christians become new persons. They are not the same anymore, for the old life is gone. A new life has begun!" (2 Corinthians 5:17).

"So let's keep focused on that goal, those of us who want everything God has for us. If any of you have something else in mind, something less than total commitment, God will clear your blurred vision—you'll see it yet!" (Philippians 3:15, THE MESSAGE).

Here are your two targets:

Love God.

Love People.

Do that.

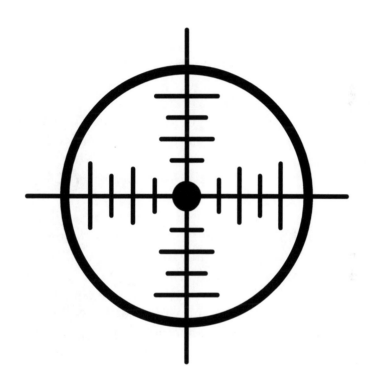

Little children, you are of God [you belong to Him] and have [already] defeated and overcome them [the agents of the antichrist], because He Who lives in you is greater (mightier) than he who is in the world.

~ *1 John 4:4,* AMP

When you go out to fight your enemies and you face horses and chariots and an army greater than your own, do not be afraid.

~ *Deuteronomy 20:1,* NLT

The LORD your God, who brought you safely out of Egypt, is with you! Before you go into battle, the priest will come forward to speak with the troops. He will say, "Listen to me, all you men of Israel! Do not be afraid as you go out to fight today! Do not lose heart or panic. For the LORD your God is going with you! He will fight for you against your enemies, and he will give you victory!

~ *Deuteronomy 20:2–9, GW, my paraphrase*

Jesus looked at them and said to them, "With men this is impossible, but with God all things are possible."

~ *Matthew 19:26,* NKJV

Daring is to be mature
when immaturity
is the "cultural cool."

Daring is to create
your life based on the
Word of God,
not the words of people.

When you let others
create your world for you,
they will always
create it too small.

DARING MEN TAKE RISKS

What Daring Men Do

Suliasi Kurulo lives in Fiji. Through his efforts and those of his team, they have seen tens of thousands of people become followers of Christ. They have built hundreds of churches in Fiji, and more than 1800 churches in more than 100 nations outside Fiji.[30] Based in one of the poorest nations on earth and fixed in the middle of the world's largest ocean, they overcame impossible circumstances to accomplish an unreasonable task. They are daring men.

When Pastor Suli's group started, theirs was a very simple desire to be daring men of God. To be like the men they read about in the Bible, Pastor Suli decided that he would present the message of Christ to everyone who lived in Fiji. His first converts decided to do it with him. That became his group.

In any nation, this is a daring dream. But in Fiji, with more than 330 islands, it was daunting. Many are very difficult to reach. They had no money to travel.

Like the daring men of history, they began with a first step, literally, down the first road.

They went door to door, village to village. Then trained others to assist in the adventure. They created methods and systems and became a thriving organization. Thousands of lives were changed. Persecution came. It was hard and lonely work as they fanned out by twos or alone to walk the island trails, yet they persisted.

The time came when they had gone to all of Fiji, but hundreds of other South Pacific islands had not heard the Good News of Jesus, particularly one dangerous place.

The island of Malaita in the Solomon Islands was home to the Kwaio tribe, and it was a lethal place. Police did not go there. Army, government workers, and fishermen who ventured there did not return. No missionary had ever returned. It was the last fierce stone-age tribe of cannibals in the South Pacific jungles.

The tribesmen on the island were in constant battle with each other. A raging spirit of death filled the beautiful south sea island.

Two of the young men from Pastor Suli's group volunteered to go. It was surely a suicide mission meant for martyrs. They gathered with men from the Solomon Islands who were also trained. The young missionaries fasted then gathered together and prayed. Tears were shed as they prayed for power and protection, then they hugged their friends and said goodbye.

The young men had to travel by canoe to get close to the island. Then they had to climb into the steep mountainous interior of the island. When two of them made contact with their first warriors, they were captured and taken to a council meeting. There, held captive in a stinking, mildewed hut with nothing more than mud for a floor, they prayed.

This was not a good moment.

Have you ever prayed over normal things, then prayed over something really critical? Was there a difference in the intensity level? Well, they began to pray, and this was one of those intense moments!

The council of chiefs called them in to find out why they were there. The young men learned through an interpreter that the high chief over that area was dying in a nearby hut, so they told the superstitious chiefs that they had brought a God with the power to heal their chief. This resonated, and the missionaries were allowed to enter the hut to go to the deathbed of the high chief.

They told the old man about Almighty God, the greatest chief in the universe. They told him of ancient writers and prophets of God, and they told him there was a way to a heavenly afterlife through Jesus Christ.

The chief listened and received Christ. The young men were jubilant. They had made a Kwaio convert! They were released to leave, and they started up the mountain paths with joy in their hearts and a great deal of relief as well. But shortly after they left the village, the high chief died. Angry warriors sprinted up the side of the mountain hunting the young men "whose god killed their chief."

They returned without finding their prey to a village filled with sad and fearful villagers. None of the Kwaio could guess what the gods might do next or who was the next to go. Two hours later, the old chief whose body was laid out in preparation for burial, started talking.

The villagers shrieked with fear, but he assured them he was OK. He told them to gather everyone and to go find the two men who had visited him. This time the warriors found the young men. The young men were terrified as they were captured and led back into the village, expecting to be killed.

In the village, the chief told the warriors not to hurt the young men. Then he gathered the tribesmen and told them, "I've been to a beautiful place. And I met a man named Moses and another named Elijah." He named names that the missionaries had never mentioned in their brief meeting with him.

The chief ended his speech with the statement, "From now on, the God of these missionaries will be the God of the Kwaio."

The next morning, the chief died. The young men began to disciple the new converts. Today, more than 90 percent of the villages in Kwaio Territory have Christian churches. I met Sova, one of the missionaries who had gone and risked everything for those islanders to hear about Jesus Christ.

This is what daring men do.

That This is a level of excitement like no other.

This is the adventure we've been called to!

The people who know
their God shall prove themselves
strong and shall stand firm
and do exploits.

~ *Daniel 11:32, AMP*

Not by the might nor
power of man,
but by My Spirit says the
Lord of hosts.

~ *Zechariah 4:6*

You shall receive power
when the Holy Spirit has come
upon you; and you shall be the
workers of my power
across the earth.

~ *Acts 1:8*

For the kingdom of God
is not just mere talk, it's about
living an empowered life.

~ *1 Corinthians 4:20*

"It takes courage to face reality, admit need, change, make decisions and hold convictions."[31]

~ Ed Cole

The Power of Seasons

One key principle that the most powerful and wealthiest men who have ever lived have mastered is this: *know your season.*

This is a key that could unlock areas of your life you've known were there but could not access.

One of the key attributes of God is a perfect sense of timing. We read throughout Scripture, "In the fullness of time." When discussing the arrival of Christ, we read, "At exactly the right time..." In other places, we read that God does things "in due season."

I remember the leader Bob Mumford years ago opening his presentation with the line, "God is slow." I know that's how we often feel!

A friend once said, "God is always right on time, but He misses some great opportunities to be early." I have felt that way for most of my life!

God is all about being successful. He really is. Highly successful. In fact, because God will have the final word and will have His way, the entire universe will become and the earth will be whatever He says it will be. Period. No discussion. Done. He said, "I will always finish what I send my word to do" (Isaiah 55:11, my paraphrase).

Yet, God put into place a system of seasons on the earth and in our lives.

You and I sense the rhythms of eternity. It surrounds our short-spanned human dramas. We see the mountains that were here when we arrived and will be here long past us, but the scope of time and eternity is hard to grasp.

We live in what is called *chronos* time. God exists in *kairos* time. *Chronos* is time within a limited framework.

Kairos is time without dimension. *Chronos* is linear. It is measured by instruments, watches, chronometers, and computers. *Kairos* is four-dimensional and exists outside the boundaries of time.

Why is this important? Because we cannot see into *kairos* time from the scope of *chronos*. Our vision into the eternal must be by our spirits, the eternal God-imaged part of our being. For the believer, that spirit has come alive and has been reconnected with God. For the man not following Christ, the spirit realm is a blur of light and speed, unfathomable, even though man has tried to look into, define, understand, and explain the supernatural from a natural perspective for centuries. The result of human effort is either frustration or false revelation.

Time management is not about the clock. We all have the same twenty-four hours no matter where we live. The clock is never the issue.

Time management is about organizing and controlling your participation in the events and seasons of life. It is about having a focus for the purpose of each minute.

Time management is about taking over ourselves, "casting down arguments and every high thing that exalts itself against the knowledge of God, *bringing every thought into captivity to the obedience of Christ*" (2 Cor. 10:5, NIV, emphasis added).

"We use our powerful God-tools for smashing warped philosophies, tearing down barriers erected against the truth of God, *fitting every loose thought and emotion and impulse into the structure of life shaped by Christ*" (2 Corinthians 10:5, THE MESSAGE, emphasis added).

God's Seasons Are Clues to His Exquisite Rhythm

Ours is a world of exquisite rhythms—the tilt of the earth; the majestic dance of the earth, moon, sun, and stars; the seasons of planting and harvest; the internal rhythms of the human body and soul; and the cycle of life.

Where I live, we have cycles of cicadas, the little grasshopper-like bugs that hibernate in the ground then appear by the millions, or so it seems, "in their season." They sit around croaking out their song according to the beat they've been given. And then they are gone again. Their season is over.

I love the rhythm of the oceans, the moon, and the tides. I sense the heartbeat of God whenever I'm near the sea. I love to experience all four seasons and to watch the dormant brown of the winter give rise to the spectacular wildflowers of spring.

The natural seasons serve to remind us that our paths, the trajectory of our lives, have seasons as well. We live life in seasons.

Jesus said to the religious people, "You can tell the seasons on earth, you know when the rainy times are coming, but the true dimension you must have is the discernment to know the seasons of the spiritual."

We are taught in Colossians to, "walk in wisdom toward them that are without, redeeming the time" (Colossians 4:5, NKJV). God says we must, "Make proper use of the season."

In the Old Testament, the prophet and daring leader Daniel wrote this:

Blessed be the name of God forever and ever, for wisdom and might are His. And He changes the times and the seasons; He removes kings and raises up kings; He gives wisdom to the wise and knowledge to those who have understanding. He reveals deep and secret things; He knows what is in the darkness, and light dwells with Him. I thank You and praise You, O God of my fathers; You have given me wisdom and might, and have now made known to me what we asked of You, for You have made known to us the king's demand.
—Daniel 2:20–23, NKJV, *emphasis added*

The prophet Jeremiah wrote, "The God who gives rain in both spring and autumn and maintains the rhythm of the seasons…" (Jeremiah 5:24, THE MESSAGE).

The real barb that hooks us is how do we recognize the season we're in and how does the season impact our lives and decisions. We don't want to plant if it's the wrong season or try to harvest if we're just scraping dead ground.

Years ago, I was producing news and documentary segments at the Super Bowl being held at the Rose Bowl Stadium in Los Angeles. I remember standing on the sidelines with the Los Angeles Rams football team. It had been an unusual season. The Rams were not expected to be in the premier game at the close of the season, on the verge of becoming champions. They didn't expect it themselves.

It had been a "lucky," or perhaps "quirky," season for them. Unusual, fortuitous events happened at every turn of the game that day, and at the end of the first half of the Super Bowl, the Rams held the lead. Jubilant at halftime, the team and the crowd realized that they had truly found themselves in the middle of a remarkable season. Victory was just two quarters away. The championship game was half won.

The second half started and the Rams fans roared. It was my first Super Bowl. I forgot the cameras and screamed with the crowd until I was hoarse. Then Terry Bradshaw brought everyone back to reality and led the Steelers to another championship by winning in convincing fashion.

Still in all, it had been a season to remember. They weren't world champions but they had gone beyond any expectation by recognizing the season and pushing as hard as possible.

Here's what Jesus said to His closest friends about seasons: "You don't need to know the time of those events that only the Father controls. But the Holy Spirit will come upon you and give you power….Then you will tell everyone about me in Jerusalem, in all Judea, in Samaria, and everywhere in the world" (Acts 1:7–8, CEV).

Jesus in essence told His guys, and tells us, "Listen, seasons will change. God sets that in order, so don't fight it. Just embrace the season you're in. And don't worry about what season is coming next. I've given you the power to be successful in *every* season!"

Rick Warren answered the question, "Why am I here?" in the mega-selling *The Purpose Driven Life*. The center of his premise was we are here for the purposes of God. Our seasons have a cohesive thread, a consistent backdrop, and no matter the season, we are here by the plan and design of Almighty God.

True Success Is to Fully Satisfy Our Personal Design

Most of my friends thought it was just a song, but God wrote it first. It's found in the third chapter of Ecclesiastes. Bob Dylan just made it famous again:

[1] To everything *there is* a season,
A time for every purpose under heaven:
[2] A time to be born, and a time to die;
A time to plant, and a time to pluck *what is* planted;
[3] A time to kill, and a time to heal;
A time to break down, and a time to build up;
[4] A time to weep, and a time to laugh;
A time to mourn, and a time to dance;
[5] A time to cast away stones, and a time to gather stones;
A time to embrace, and a time to refrain from embracing;
[6] A time to gain, and a time to lose;
A time to keep, and a time to throw away;
[7] A time to tear, and a time to sew;
A time to keep silence, and a time to speak;
[8] A time to love, and a time to hate;
A time of war, and a time of peace.
—NKJV

We live by seasons. It is not always harvest time. It is not always the time to be urgently busy. We must adapt to the season.

We cannot live by another man's season. We cannot write a book because the other guy did. We cannot sell our car because the other guy got a new one. We have to live in and adapt to our own season. We will have seasons of plenty and seasons of strife.

The seasons always change. Change is the one constant you will always have. Have you ever taken a two-week trip, been away from home, returned back, and it seemed like so many things changed? When we're in the middle of the change, the subtleties of change mask the depth.

Paul taught Timothy, "Preach the word of God. Be prepared, whether the time is favorable or not. Patiently correct, rebuke, and encourage your people with good teaching" (2 Timothy 4:2, NLT).

Paul said be patient, but always preach the Word. The Word of God is never off-season. We always dwell on and share God's Word, whether it's in season or out of season. We will be accepted at times and rejected at times.

When you're in a tough season, here's the promise of His presence: "For we are God's workmanship, created in Christ Jesus to do good works, which God prepared in advance for us to do" (Ephesians 2:10, NIV).

When we keep going and keep doing those works according to His purposes, we are sure to have success through every season.

We are here on
purpose for His purposes.
He promises over and
over He will be with us.
When we follow Him,
we follow Him to our
destiny and to a
successful life.

You cannot change
the season, but you can
change what you do
in the season.

You cannot change
the past, but you can
change the future.
Decide to change your
future by not limiting
yourself to your past.

Decisions made while
looking back
will not take
you forward.

Daring Men Recognize the Season

Recognizing the season of life we've entered is key to successful living. Timing is the critical ingredient in success.

Hitting a homerun in baseball is good. Thousands of men have done that. But when New York Giants outfielder Bobby Thomson came to bat on October 3, 1951, against the Brooklyn Dodgers, the game was on the line, the season in the balance, and runners in scoring position.[32] If he fails, it's over and they lose. And, at that moment, he hits a homerun. Hitting a homerun during practice on a back lot was great. Hitting a homerun in that moment went down in the annals of history. That's the timing that makes heroes.

Here are a few tips to recognize your season and act toward success.

First: Measure Your Life

Using the Word of God as a standard, ask yourself, "Where am I in my journey? What man has faced before what I'm facing now? Where am I in my fight to be Christlike as a man? Whose story in Scripture most resonates with me today?"

"What are my dreams, and where am I in my pursuit of them?"

"What is the reality of my life?"

Assess where you really are. When asked about how good his teams are, football coach Bill Parcells simply replied, "You are what your win-loss record says you are."[33] You are what your Bible measures you out to be.

A word of caution, listen: DO NOT measure your life against the lives of others. The sin of comparison will lead you to pride, misgivings, arrogance, or despair. The dangerous sin of comparison stopped Israel repeatedly as they must have reasoned, "Well, at least we're not as bad as the Canaanites."

If you measure your life against others, you will always have a moving target for a goal. It's a sure-fired way to live a life of frustration, which means it is not smart.

Second: Be Filled with the Holy Spirit

Jesus said we would have discernment, ability to assess situations and seasons when the Holy Spirit is in us.

Discernment is a natural gift to many women, particularly moms. A "mother's intuition" is legendary. They seem to know exactly what their child is really telling them. They know the lies and they sense the truth.

The infilling of the Holy Spirit will grant you perspective. God's Spirit gives you the ability to get above an issue and see the larger picture. This is what coaches in sports have from a lofted box in the stadium or standing back on a sideline gathering in the full picture.

Habakkuk wrote, "I've gone up to a high place to get perspective. So that from that place, I can write the vision and we can run full speed toward the goal" (Habakkuk 2:2).

Perspective allows you to run fast. However, without the quiet discerning moments of getting the perspective of God's heart, you'll keep running but collapse from exhaustion or run into an immovable object.

Let the Holy Spirit lead you and you'll run to win, while taking time to rest and relate to others.

Third: Be Faithful

Faithfulness builds character. Be faithful to your word, be faithful to others, and be faithful to God's Spirit.

I think of my friend Dino who found himself in a difficult job situation, with advice coming from every angle. Wise men told him a series of conflicting things to do—stay, leave, overthrow leadership, submit to leadership, rebuke, and run. He stayed faithful to the calling of God on his life. He honored the leadership God had put into his life for that season.

He and his wife took a breath, got away, and removed themselves from the heat of the fire for some time. Then they made their decision. They made a choice consistent with honor to those in relation to him in his passing season. It was faithful to the Word of God and covered with respect for leaders, whether they had been making right decisions or not. He moved forward.

With the help of friends, they launched a new church, one that had a unique perspective on helping others. Today it's one of the most influential churches in the nation, if not the world. He made a choice based on faithfulness to the Lord, the church, and his integrity.

Now that same spirit of loyalty, honor, and faithfulness is what Dino is reaping with incredible leaders around him like Marc, Johnny, Mike, Dan, Derek, and hundreds of strong men! Honor births loyalty.

Faithfulness in your season births greatness in life.

Fourth: Ask God for Wisdom

You can't escape it, because wisdom is the architect. Wisdom gives us strategy and strategy brings us to victory. James exposed an extremely important revelation for you and me: "If any of you lacks wisdom, let him ask of God, who gives to all liberaly and without reproach" (James 1:5, NKJV).

Remember the key: We need wisdom, which is the application of knowledge and understanding, and we get it from God. To get it, He says, "JUST ASK ME FOR IT!"

It's not the school you've gone to, the courses you've taken, or the books you've read. God says, "You don't have to qualify to ask Me. JUST ASK ME!"

Fifth: Think, Reflect, Plan—Then Act

I've been "pitched" at least a thousand times. I've read the prospectus, seen the PowerPoint, watched the video, monitored the reports, shifted my paradigm, and tried to get in touch with my inner wild man in order to stay up with the presenter.

In Christian circles, I've seen and heard enough plans to evangelize the earth that, if anyone had done them, we'd have run out of people decades ago and had to fund Mars settlements just to try to find someone to evangelize.

After seeing hundreds of great plans on paper and hearing thousands of great ideas, I can tell you that the only ones I've ever seen that were successful are the ones the man went out and started.

Don't get caught up in a cycle of thinking, analyzing, praying, and conceiving. Birth it!

Seth Godin says, "Thanks for all the great ideas and corporate breakthroughs on paper. What have you shipped?"[34]

Start the church. Launch the website. Build the gym. Marry the woman, c'mon brother! Crank the engine! Let's move! Go!

You can grind to inertia due to paralysis by analysis. Read the season, but don't drown in it. Read it facing forward. Make a decision, limit the risk, and then, either move forward or abandon it altogether. It is the power of God that will make it come to pass anyway. Just let it go. Breathe life into it or let...it...die.

"In a moment of crisis the best thing is to make the right decision. The worst thing is to make no decision at all."[35] ~ Teddy Roosevelt

Sixth: Focus on Principle Not Conditions

Conditions will change, storms will be here and be gone, the external will forever be in flux, but the principles of God never change. Decisions must be made from an inner faith and strength, not from an outward earthly source.

And here's another word of caution: NEVER MAKE MAJOR DECISIONS IN TIMES OF DESPAIR.

Recognize the weak moments, and stay away from choices that will limit your life, change your course, or affect others deeply.

The time to make major choices is in the season of strength. That's when you join the gym, hire the trainer, or get a habit going so that when you're weak, it's already part of your life. Kicking porn must be done in times of strength, but at that moment when you're strong, put the fences in place that will protect you when you're weak. Put the computer in the kitchen, sign on to web protector, get a prayer partner, seek wise counsel, and tear up the hidden credit cards. Make the wise decisions when you're strong!

Adapt your thinking and decision-making to the season.

Len Sweet observed, "You're either in a storm in life, or you've just been in a storm… and, then, you're actually about ready to head into a storm again!"[36] Seasons change. Adapt to them.

"Things seem to turn out best for those who make the best of how things turn out."[37]

~ John Wooden, legendary coach

Seven: Fix Your Course

Make a decision, and then manage the decision. Go after the direction that you've set as your course with the intent of capture. Put your faith in Almighty God, then pursue it.

"But before all these things, they will lay their hands on you and persecute you, delivering you up to the synagogues and prisons. You will be brought before kings and rulers for My name's sake. But it will turn out for you as an occasion for testimony. Therefore settle it in your hearts not to meditate beforehand on what you will answer; for I will give you a mouth and wisdom which all your adversaries will not be able to contradict or resist."

~ *Luke 21:12–15,* NKJV

Follow God no matter what.

> *Delight yourself also in the* LORD,
> *And He shall give you the desires of your heart.*
> *Commit your way to the* LORD,
> *Trust also in Him,*
> *And He shall bring it to pass....*
> *The steps of a good man are ordered by the* LORD,
> *And He delights in his way.*
> *Though he fall, he shall not be utterly cast down;*
> *For the* LORD *upholds him with His hand.*
> *~ Psalm 37:4–5, 23–24 NKJV*

There is a deep abiding peace for those in Christ that is beyond the reach of any season.

Your God is the same God who delivered Daniel from the lions, the same God who delivered Israel from slavery and made them wealthy, the same God who multiplied the fishes and loaves, the same God who led Abraham to his destiny, the same God who gave Samson great strength and the same God who raised Jesus from the grave of death to life for you and me!

He is the same God yesterday, today and forever!

The sum total of your life is not about the season you're in.

It's about the reason you're here.

You're here for the pleasure of God.

Rest in His grace, and go be daring.

DARING MEN
DIE TO SELF

Humility - Daring Men

It had been an elegant gala at the impressive Washington, DC, Sheraton. The U.S. President had spoken that morning. Famous world leaders and national political leaders had gathered to honor key Christian leaders that evening. I was heading from a VIP gathering over to the massive ballroom where our company had just produced a national television special. The Washington, DC, elite were already gathering in a spectacular penthouse suite for an after-event reception, the lights of the capitol glittering below.

I stopped by prior to the reception to check on my camera crews and wrap-up teams. Cleaning crews had already swarmed into the room like locusts. Tables were stripped of covers and the glamorous stage sat naked in the glare of blue-white work lights. I rounded a corner, looking, checking, and making sure we'd left nothing behind. Instead, I found a sight I will never forget.

Bill Bright was there—*the* Bill Bright, the founder and president of the largest Christian ministry in the world, double the size financially of any American denomination, the "Bill Gates" of Christian ministry in his generation. Bill was still at the center table where he'd been seated during the event. Only now, he's not there with the famous or noted. He's sitting alone with the Dominican busboy that had served his table. And lovingly and patiently, with his complete focus on the young man, he was sharing the love of Christ, the story of a Savior and the joy of knowing God.

Bill Bright was supposed to be at the reception with the big shots. There was no staff with him, no cameras or reporters. It wasn't a photo op. It was a man sitting alone who didn't care about anything but people coming to Christ. Bill Bright was a daring leader. He knew the secret of true humility.

It's been said, "Humility is not thinking less of yourself, but thinking of yourself less." Anonymity is the essence of true humility.

Daring men dare to
make a difference.

It doesn't have to
be eloquent or clever or
noticed, it's simply truth
held in the heart,
and acted on.

This is what daring
men do, period.

Daring Grace - Jonah

The story of Jonah was most often told me as a young boy this way: "Here's what will happen if you disobey God." The last thing I wanted was to mess up and have God throw me into the mouth of a whale! If I did the wrong thing, messed up, lied, or did something bad, it may not be a whale, but God would GET ME somehow, and a fish might even look good compared to what else He could do.

That, my friend, is error. "I don't want to be a Jonah, and be swallowed by a whale" is a song you never want to hear your kids sing. It distorts Scripture.

The story of Jonah is the story of God's amazing grace, His provision for humanity, and His longsuffering with His followers. God was all about bringing His love to a city, Ninevah, that did not love Him, did not want His love, and turned their backs on Him, preferring their own gods and ways to the God of the universe.

The short version of the story is that Jonah is a prophet of God in Israel. God tells him to go to a wicked, pagan city called Ninevah and tell them about God's love for them, and His provision of grace so they can be rescued from damnation.

Jonah doesn't want to go. He's heard of them and doesn't think they deserve saving. He fears their vicious attitudes, so he gets on a boat headed the other way. A major storm threatens to sink the ship. The sailors jettison their cargo to lighten the ship and pray to their gods for safety. Finally, Jonah tells them, "I'm the reason there's a storm. I am running from God." Then he makes the offer. To save them, they can throw him overboard. They do. The storm stops.

Jonah gets swallowed by a large fish, perhaps a whale. In there for three days, he changes his mind, prays for forgiveness, and asks God to let him live. The fish vomits him onto the beach, he goes to Ninevah, and he tells them about God. The city is transformed and the spiritual victory is won.

Now, consider if this is the judgment of God or the grace of God. Is the fish judgment or grace? That can be found in the answer to this question...

How old is the fish?

The Bible says Jonah was swallowed by a fish that God "had prepared" (Jonah 1:17, AMP). God is a God of process. He will use the natural processes of life to our benefit, for our provision. How old was the fish?

Before Jonah had ever made his decision, before he ever made the wrong choice, before he ever got on the boat going in the wrong direction, and before he ever told the crew they could throw him out to save themselves, God had prepared the way of escape for him. God had placed in the middle of that storm the means to help Jonah make a new choice, the right choice, and get back on track.

The fish wasn't judgment. The fish was grace. That fish was God's provision in the storm to keep Jonah from drowning and from killing himself through a bad decision. His life was rescued by the whale.

In the middle of the storm, God was all about fulfilling the strategy He had to rescue Jonah, put him back on course as a prophet and fulfill Jonah's destiny!

God's unmerited favor is His provision of strength for us to live righteously. His grace is massive!

Religion is all about your past. Grace is all about your future!

Religion is a push-down model. "You should do this." "You shouldn't do that." "You better act like this." "Don't you dare do that." It creates condemnation and obligation. It keeps us looking down at where we are or back at where we've been.

God, however, is the "one who lifts up my head" (Psalm 3:3, NKJV).

The things of God take us up, not down.

Following Christ is about looking up at where we're going.

Following Christ is not about obligation or works.

Jesus said it this way: "Because I AM, YOU ARE!"

Because of *His* righteousness, *we* are called "the righteousness of God, through faith, in Jesus Christ" (Romans 3:22, NKJV).

Because of *His* strength, we can say, "*I* can do all things through Christ who strengthens me" (Philippians 4:13, NKJV).

Jesus told His disciples that we would do greater things, that by His Spirit, we can declare over ourselves, our families, our businesses, our churches, and our nations: "Greater is He that is in [us], than [the enemy] that is in the world" (1 John 4:4, KJV).

Christ says, "Because I AM, You Are!"

Life in Christ creates freedom, joy, energy, and an uplifted spirit.

God's mercy delivers us from our past, and His grace empowers us toward our future. We learn from the past. It's a resource, not a dead weight. We are not bound by it.

We see the huge grace of God at the start of the third chapter of Jonah: *"Then the Lord spoke to Jonah a second time."* God did not quit on Jonah! If Jonah had messed up again, we may have seen a sentence in the fourth chapter stating, "And the Lord spoke to Jonah a third time…" His grace is inexhaustible! God will not quit on you.

How old is your fish? If Jonah had not voluntarily left the boat, he'd have never found God's provision waiting for him in the storm. Trust in the Lord. He loves you and He is for you…and He will not stop being for you! Ever.

*Blessed are the daring men who trust in the Lord
and have made the Lord their hope and confidence.
They are like trees planted along a riverbank, with
roots that reach deep into the water.
They are not bothered by the heat or worried by
long months of drought.
Their leaves stay green, and they never stop
producing fruit.*
~ *Jeremiah 17:5–8,* NLT

God's grace is the fuel to be daring.
His grace is your fish in the storm.
His plan is for your ultimate success.

I love you, LORD; you
are my strength.

The LORD is my rock, my fortress,
and my savior; My God is my rock, in
whom I find protection.

He is my shield, the power
that saves me,
and my place of safety.

I called on the LORD, who is
worthy of praise,
and he saved me from my enemies.

You have armed me with
strength for the battle,
You have subdued my enemies
under my feet.

~ Psalm 18:1–3, 39, NLT

"If you know the enemy
and know yourself, you
need not fear the result of
a hundred battles.

If you know yourself but
not the enemy, for every
victory gained you will also
suffer a defeat.

If you know neither the
enemy nor yourself, you will
succumb in every battle."[38]

- Sun Tzu
From The Art of War

The Hinge of History

The amazing story of Christian David is one that befits a legend, but few have ever heard his name. He changed the course of human history, yet there are no books about him and no plaques or memorials hung in his honor. What you're about to read has largely been overlooked.

Yet his story is our story, and it is remarkable.[39]

Christian was a nondescript young man in the middle ages, a day-worker. He was a young man looking for more from his spiritual life, but not sure where to find it. He just tried to eke out life in desperate times. Then he met some men who knew Christ in a vibrant fashion.

He connected.

Our lives are the result of connecting with someone else—the person who told us about Christ, the guy who got us our first job, the teacher who encouraged us to think, the parent who challenged us to greatness, and the pastor who filled our hearts with the love of Christ. We're all connected to someone who connected us to where we are today.

An entire village was transformed when Jesus met a woman at a well. What seemed like a moment of chance for her and a moment of strategic fulfillment for the Lord was actually the day she became a hinge of history for her village and for Samaria (John 4).

She meets Jesus, her life is changed, and she goes and tells everyone else. Years later when the disciple Philip first goes to Samaria, he finds people already with the seed of the Gospel, eager to receive. The disciple sends word to Jerusalem, "Send more ministers, there's an awakening happening here!"

Where did that come from? A woman in a "chance" encounter with Christ became the "connector" for an entire region that years later had remarkable revival.

We are all connectors, for good or for bad.

We all have the potential to connect future generations to the life of Christ and the power of His presence we walk in today.

Today we sit on the shoulders of those who came before us. We sing their songs, read their books, and live in the nations they built.

Christian David was a hinge of history.

You can be, too.

Over six hundred years ago, there was a period of history when the corporate church controlled most of the culture. It was called the "Dark Ages." A man in Prague, Czechoslovakia named Jan Hus stood up against the tyrannical leadership of the religious establishment.

Jan declares that people should know the Bible and that they can be saved "by faith." Parallel to that, John Wycliffe in England is producing the first Bibles that people could actually acquire. The Bible had been solely in the hands of the professional religious leaders for hundreds of years. "Common" people had no access until now.

Jan Hus is influential. His words of freedom in Christ begin to stir the hearts of people across Europe.

Leaders whose position derives from control of providing "salvation" to whomever they wish, take exception. They decide to get rid of Jan Hus. In 1415, they lure him to a meeting in Constanze, Germany, and while hundreds of religious leaders look on, they burn him at the stake.

As he burns, he declares, "Within one hundred years there will be a man that rises up, whom you will not be able to silence."

In 1450, Guttenberg's press becomes operational, and by the 1500s Bibles are being produced by the thousands.

Almost exactly a century after Jan's death, in 1517, Martin Luther begins the revolution of thought that never stops. The Reformation kicks in. A new awakening of faith in Christ explodes around the world. The world changes irreversibly.

When Jan Hus was killed, his followers were attacked relentlessly by armies of the institutional church. Many of his followers were chased across Europe and settled into areas off the beaten path to be safe.

One group near Jan's hometown was chased into the caves and valleys around the Moravia River. They established homes and scratched out a living, keeping the freedom of grace and faith alive in their hearts.

Three hundred years after Jan's death, a young man name Christian David is working as a handyman, a transient carpenter in Germany. He spends his days working and his free time searching the Scriptures for truth. He is restless, business is not good, and his spirit is unsettled. How can he connect with Christ with a vibrant joy? He's just not satisfied with the answers from the old priests and teachers that give him rules and regulations.

Looking for work, he travels into the Moravia River valley.

It is there that he meets men that take him into a new, fresh vibrant faith in Christ—a faith based on grace and faith, not works and penance.

Christian is fired up! He finally feels like a free man, full of joy and a sense of purpose in his life, a zeal to tell others! He's connected.

Count Zinzendorf is born in 1700 to a wealthy family in Dresden. They have massive landholdings and great influence. Excelling in academics, he quickly becomes a lawyer and by the age of twenty-one is practicing before the highest levels of government.

In 1722, a young handyman is introduced to him. The count puts Christian David to work on the estate. Some time later they get into conversation. Christian tells Zinzendorf about his faith in Christ, the freedom of faith, and the joy of walking in grace. Zinzendorf is captivated. He's found real truth that so often eluded him in religion and law.

Christian David then tells him of the persecuted Christians living in caves and poor farms in the vicinity of the Moravian River.

Count Zinzendorf makes a historic invitation. If Christian will go get the people, the count will give them land on which to build and grounds on which to farm. The Moravians arrive and build a city that still exists in modern Germany, Hernhut. Today it is the site of the European headquarters for Youth With A Mission.

The Moravians practice powerful times of prayer. Sometimes their prayer meetings continue for an entire evening. Zinzendorf joins their prayer meetings. And then, something breaks.

In the summer of 1727, they're in prayer and it goes all night—not uncommon. But then it continues the next day, then another day and night until it goes for months. People come from across Europe. Many are healed. Many experience the presence of the Holy Spirit. Many come to new faith in Christ. It is remarkable!

That famous prayer meeting lasts for one hundred years.

Out of that prayer meeting comes a strong sense of taking the gospel to other nations. What is normal today in missionary outreaches did not exist in that age. But, as they pray, the pull becomes stronger, drawing them out.

One day, two former slaves from St. Thomas Island hear about the meeting and travel to attend it. They tell of the deplorable conditions of the slaves, the occult practices, and the darkness of spirit.

Two German men are so moved that they walk to the center of the room and declare they are going to St. Thomas. The group prays over them and sends them out. They discover the only way to reach the slaves is for themselves also to become slaves. So they sell themselves into slavery to bring the gospel. These are the first missionaries of the new Christian era.

The pull for missions becomes an overwhelming call. Zinzendorf becomes the first man to bring the gospel to the native people of the American English colonies. Now teams are crossing the seas to take Christ to the nations.

John Wesley is a young British preacher who wants to make his mark in the colonies. He sets out for America in 1735. The trip is marked by terrible weather. Storms threaten to sink the sailing ship. The entire crew and travelers are sick, depressed, and panicked, except for a small group of people deep in the bow rooms of the ship. Wesley marks in his journal that they pray, sing, and thank God for safe passage. It is a group of Moravians from Hernhut.

Wesley has a disastrous time in America. Nothing goes as he hopes. He returns after three difficult years broken, humbled, and, as he wrote his brother Charles, "perhaps without any faith at all."

On May 24, 1738, Wesley hears about a prayer meeting in an area of London called Aldersgate. It's the Moravians! Some of the same group of people he had met on the ship in the storm—the ones who had kept faith.

He attends the prayer meeting, writing later that he sensed the presence of God run through his body. It was "strangely warm." "It pleased God," he wrote later, "to kindle a fire which I trust shall never be extinguished." Faith, grace, and joy fills his heart.

Wesley launches his ministry again, but now it is full of power, life, and freedom. Hundreds and then thousands of people come to Christ. Over the next fifty years, John Wesley's books sell millions of copies, the nation experiences transformation, and a movement is birthed.

A twenty-six-year-old man, Francis Asbury, sits enthralled in Wesley's weekly meeting in 1771. Wesley asks if someone will answer the call to go to America. It is a godless place, with many hardships, but needs the gospel.

Francis immediately volunteers. George Washington writes in his journals late in life, that if it were not for the faith and preaching of Francis Asbury, the newly formed United States of America may not have survived.

From 1771 until 1816, almost forty-five years, Asbury travels by horseback on the roughest roads, sleeps in gritty straw corners, and eats whatever anyone has to offer. From the Atlantic to the Appalachians, from Maine to the Gulf of Mexico, traveling over three hundred thousand miles, and preaching twenty thousand sermons, Francis proclaims the gospel. At one point he writes in his journal, "How nice it would be to have just a solid wooden board to sleep on." He sees hundreds of thousands come to Christ.

Asbury never owns a home or anything of value, other than some Bibles and a saddle. In his last days, so torn are his feet from years in the stirrups that people have to carry him to the front of churches and sit him on a table so he can lovingly speak of his Savior.

Asbury is open to all people. His ministry includes slaves, foreigners, and the marginal fringe of culture. In Washington, DC, he meets personally with George Washington. He leads Richard Bassett, a signer of the U.S. Constitution, to Christ. Bassett frees his slaves and pays them as hired laborers. In Philadelphia, Asbury helps launch the African Methodist Episcopal Church. By the time Asbury dies, the Methodist Church in America begun by Asbury's mentor John Wesley grows from three hundred members to over two hundred thousand.

Harry Hoosier, a former slave, is one of the men who travels with Asbury. Hoosier has enormous lungs and can speak to thousands without a microphone. He also has an enormous spirit and anointing, and thousands are saved yearly during his ministry. It is not acceptable to many to see a white Englishman riding with this freed slave. The people who follow Harry's ministry come to be called a derisive nickname, "Hoosiers." But, so great is his impact that today, the state of Indiana in the USA carries the motto, "The Hoosier State."

These are daring men, the ones who started the circuit-riding preachers, telling all who will listen about Jesus. They speak to settlers and slaves, bankers and bartenders, governors and gangsters, and change the course of a nation.

"Francis Asbury is entitled to rank as one of the builders of our nation."[40]
~ President Calvin Coolidge

Christian David is the "hinge of history" in this story. John Hus' word on faith and grace was lost in the caves of Moravia, but Christian David brings the Moravians to Zinzendorf. That prayer meeting launches world missions and travels to London, where Wesley finds his vibrant faith. Wesley's missionaries cover the world. In particular, Asbury comes from that meeting, and his ministry rescues the soul of a new nation called the United States of America.

Christian David is a laborer with just a hammer in his hand. Yet he becomes the hinge for altering the course of human history.

The world defines men by what is in their hand—job, money, influence, power, position. God defines men by what is in their heart—faith, grace, endurance, fortitude, anointing, vision.

God will use what is in your hand, to fulfill what He put in your heart.

For the man who is the follower of Christ, what is in your hand will be the tool God uses to fulfill what He has put in your heart.

The Bible says that a man's gift makes room for him (Proverbs 18:16). Christian David could have despised being just a mere day laborer, an itinerant worker with a hammer, but he committed his whole life and what was in his hand to service to Christ. What was in his hand changed the course of history.

Moses had been a prince in Egypt and was raised in the Pharoah's house, but now he was just a desert shepherd with no future and no hope. Just a shepherd carrying a staff. But when God spoke to him, he took that shepherds' staff back to Egypt, and it became a tool to set God's people free, to part the Red Sea, bring water from a rock, and lead a nation to their destiny.

If you're a teacher, be a great teacher. If a manager, be excellent at it. If a chef, be an award-winning chef. The Bible says to do everything to the fullest of our ability (Ecclesiastes 9:10)!

John Hus put something into motion. He was willing to lay his life down for the next generation. What you do with your life is important, but the most important part is what you put into motion.

What price are you willing to pay to change the history of your family? Your city? Your nation?

> *I know how to be abased, and I know how to abound. Everywhere and in all things I have learned both to be full and to be hungry, both to abound and to suffer need. I can do all things through Christ who strengthens me.*
> ~ **Philippians 4:12–13,** NKJV

You can do everything God placed you on the earth to do. Be faithful to what God puts in your hand, and He will be faithful to fulfill what is in your heart.

You CAN do your destiny!! Daring men die to self to pursue life in Christ.

For I am not
ashamed of this
Good News about
Christ. It is the
power of God
at work, saving
everyone who
believes.

~ Romans 1:16, NLT

The Daring Man - Daniel

Daniel was a daring man. He faced the pain of prison, the danger of a lions' den, the bitter hurts of slavery, and the devastation of losing his family. He was taken prisoner as a young man to Babylon. Ripped from his homeland and marched through the desert to a foreign place where people neither knew him nor his God, he decided to adapt to the new season, but not by compromising his faith in God.

Daniel made an early stand against the pagan rituals at his forced schooling. His friends stood against idolatry and survived being thrown into a heated furnace.

Daniel lived in a nation so perverse that when we describe places or cities with ungodly cultures we say it has "the spirit of Babylon." Yet, Daniel lived as a faithful follower of God in the middle of this massively unrighteous nation.

And Daniel didn't just live there, but he also thrived there. He prophetically rescued the nation from famine and became one of the country's great leaders and one of the top leader's chief advisors. Daniel presided over one of the most perverse cultures that has ever existed, yet he never succumbed to it and he never left!

Daniel was a strong man in tough times. He was resolute in spirit and disciplined in his habits. He prayed, ate the right diet, and was bold in talking about his God. He never backed off.

The old proverb is that an acorn when put in the ground doesn't become dirt. It becomes a tree. Be like Daniel, bold in your confession of Christ, and not shaped by the culture around you.

Daniel lived in Babylon, but the spirit of Babylon never lived in him.

Daring in Transition

One of the books that I most often refer to in talking to men about life's obstacles and changes is *Never Quit* written by my dad, Ed Cole. He rewrote it and repackaged it three times until he got it the way he wanted it. Decades later, it is still selling by the thousands.

In it, he shares a dynamic pattern of leaving past issues and moving to the next level of life. It is a guide to victorious transition. His premise is that we really only do two things in life: we enter and we leave. Enter school, leave school; enter a job, leave a job; enter a relationship, leave a relationship. And what we do as we leave determines how successful we will be when we enter our new season.

As we move through our lives, making changes, following our plan, and drawing closer to our destiny, we will suffer the accompanying crisis. That's normal. Abnormal would be if we made all our changes, they were easy, no one noticed, and those who did notice were thrilled, including all the devils of hell. Crisis is normal.

In the change and flux of life, remember that "God always works for our highest good" (Romans 8:28, my paraphrase). His Spirit never departs from us, even when we are at our lowest ebb. He does not reject us, never turns His back on us. In fact, He put it in writing: "Even when we are too weak to have any faith left, he remains faithful to us and will help us, for he cannot disown us who are part of himself, and he will always carry out his promises to us" (2 Timothy 2:13, TLB).

Or, as my dad phrased it, "God will not deny us because for Him to do so, would be to deny Himself."

Going through changes? Transitioning out of one job into another? Suffered the humiliation of a bankruptcy, failed at marriage, got arrested and it really was your fault? God is right there with you in the middle of it.

Here are ten directives to create success in your life. These will stand the test of time. They have proven to be extremely powerful when applied. That doesn't mean they're easy, it means they work.

1. Crisis is NORMAL to life.

Recognize that crisis is normal. The only thing you're sure of as you mature is that there will be change. True change comes only by way of crisis. It is not something that happens *to* you. It is part of life. Embrace it, and learn to make it work *for* you.

2. Follow God's pattern, first FORGIVE.

The essence of the greatness of Christ is that He forgave. Remember, the "enemies," those who hurt you, actually moved God's plan forward in your life. That's what Judas did for Jesus. "Rejoice and be exceedingly glad," the scripture reads, when people persecute and misuse you (Matthew 5:11–12). Those people really did you a favor. Flush it all out of your system. Forgive them all.

Let the words of Joseph to his scheming, betraying, and murderous brothers be your words too: "Am I God, to judge and punish you? As far as I am concerned, *God turned into good what you meant for evil*, for he brought me to this high position I have today so that I could save the lives of many people" (Genesis 50:20, TLB).

3. Confess that God is your SOURCE.

We don't look to our jobs, our sales figures, the stock exchange, or our own strength, but we look to God. He is the source of wealth, wisdom, and eternal life. Confess it out loud until it becomes part of your life's steady rhythms and the "self-talk" in your head.

4. Don't panic.

Poor decisions come from panic. Stress will kill initiative and break relationships. Keep God's peace in your heart. Stay productive. When you get fired, pick up the phone and call a friend and ask for a job. Keep moving.

5. Embrace the SOVEREIGNTY of God.

He is the God of the entire universe, all that exists. And, He will win. God's Word is filled from beginning to end with stories of men just like you who faced the crisis of transition and, no matter what it was, God turned it around for good in their lives. Embrace that He will win one for you.

6. Don't limit God.

Faith does not limit God, and God does not limit faith. How far you expect God's presence to go is how far you're going to go. When you limit yourself, you limit God. And when you limit God, you limit yourself. He knows. Expect God to act.

7. HUMBLE yourself to obey God.

We must recognize that God's principles are immutable. We humble ourselves to obey His word, because it is life. We admit that we don't know it all, haven't seen it all, and can't do it all.

DARING MEN DIE TO SELF

8. **Trust God to VINDICATE you.**

The Bible teaches us that God is the one who has the scales and measures of life. He is the one who will fight for you. When you read the Old Testament, when someone else put their hand on God's people, He was ruthless in protecting His family. If you have legal issues, find the best legal mind you can. Don't ignore it, but trust that God will lead you to the right person, and empower you to make wise judgments.

9. **Don't stop COMMUNICATING.**

Answer the phone. Text people back. Don't succumb to a "cave mentality." No matter how many people are talking about you, they are not *always* talking about you. They're living their lives. Come out! You will never see the light until you're out of the cave.

10. **Base your actions on PRINCIPLE.**

Men with principles do not wilt under pressure. If your choices are based on preference or position or the plaudits of men, your foundation is cracked. Pressure doesn't make a man. It reveals a man for who he really is. Find the truths of God and make that your foundation.

Act on Your Smallest Possible

Oral Roberts taught on the importance of faith, and the power of the Holy Spirit in a believer's life. One of his famous quotes is:

**"If you miss seeing the invisible,
you will not be able to do the impossible."[41]**

Oral Roberts is the man who taught us that "God is a good God." Because of that, he said, "Something good is going to happen to you." He also made famous the admonition, "Expect a miracle!"

I was healed in an Oral Roberts crusade when I was five years old. I had limited hearing in my left ear. Mom and Dad walked me up the long plywood ramp to a man sitting on a folding chair. He prayed for me, and instantly I was healed. My eyes aren't as good as when I was younger, my back sometimes hurts, I can't lift as much, but I think my hearing just may be perfect for the rest of my life.

This is important: to see things in faith. Trusting God is first a matter of the heart, then comes confession, and then you take action. The smallest action will create the largest results. Mom and Dad had a sick kid, no money and no insurance, and just did what they could to find help. Reduced in options to their smallest possible act, they simply did that smallest possible.

What happened was never a source of pride. No one ever talked about it again in our family. Hardly any act could have been smaller than driving to a meeting and walking up to the front. Yet it produced impossible, miraculous results.

*The impossible happens when the smallest
possible is acted on.*

Daring by Definition

Definitions give us the action pictures that our mind uses to make decisions. We make decisions based on faith and belief, even if they are wrong. So, wrong definitions cause wrong decisions.

In fact, we define our own lives by our words, actions, thoughts, friendships, endurance, and all the ingredients of our character.

Now here's the rub…

What you allow to define you will determine your destiny.

When we use the Word of God to define us, it opens to us the possibility of being a daring man… When we let the world define us, it keeps us bound to a life of mediocre natural living.

Now, let's look at a definition of our lives as men, and compare that to the life of King David.

A Daring Man Pursues God

If you lived in Bible days, would you want to be one of King David's closest friends and advisers? Would you want to live just a stone's throw from his palace and enjoy unlimited access? Would you want to do that and have a really, really, really good-looking wife, too? Think again.

One of David's closest friends, advisors, and most valiant warriors had a gorgeous wife, and it got him killed. David, described as the man "after God's own heart," had huge issues in his life. The Bible is brutally honest. We know things about David that perhaps none of his closest friends even knew.

David saw Bathsheba, his friend Uriah's wife, and lusted for her. Sure, she was married to his friend, but perhaps it was a sense of entitlement that caused David to call for her. After all, he was the king.

She became pregnant while her husband Uriah was off fighting the war, where David was supposed to be. So, David called Uriah off the battlefield, hoping to pass the baby off as Uriah's. But Uriah was a noble man and didn't feel right sleeping in his own bed while his men were fighting, so he slept under the stars.

This ruined David's plan. So he made his next move and arranged for Uriah to be killed in battle.

Yes, David murdered, made mistakes, and did terrible things. He fought savage wars and killed lions with his bare hands. He was a bloody man. Yet David was held in high esteem by God. God uses dozens of songs David wrote as part of His Word to mankind. God uses David as an example of a faithful warrior. God made His Son, Jesus, part of David's lineage.

In the Book of Acts in the New Testament, we read, "After David had done the will of God in his own generation, he died and was buried with his ancestors" (Acts 13:36, NLT). God wrote the Bible, and God wrote this scripture.

God says about this guy, who made so many mistakes and killed his best friend to steal his wife, "He did everything I wanted him to." *What? How can this be?*

THE GRACE OF GOD IS MASSIVE!

God is full of mercy and grace. He was that way with David, and His heart is that way toward you. You are not seen in the light of your human imperfections, but through the filter of the righteousness of Jesus Christ. That's how much God loves you. That's how great His grace is for you.

How did David merit such words? Here's the answer: David's heart was toward God. In spite of his imperfections, his humanity, and his sin-disease, David had a heart that constantly yearned for, turned to, and leaned into the heart of Almighty God.

Lean into God. Face forward, turning to Him. God loves you passionately. He's for you, not against you!

What does it mean to pursue the pleasure of God's presence? It means to have a heart that constantly yearns for, turns to, leans into the heart of Almighty God.

Read that again. Get it in your spirit: God loves you and knows you will make mistakes. Yet His mercy and grace and forgiveness are turned toward you, even right now. Whatever place you are at today, regardless of how big a mess you have made in the past, depending on what you do right now, God can still one day say of you, "He did everything I wanted him to do."

I am not defined
as a man
by the things
I struggle with.

I am defined as a
man by the fact that
I am a passionate
pursuer of the
pleasure of
His presence.

A Brother Is Daring for His Brothers

In our culture, there's a word used to refer to getting connected—*networking*. To be "networked" with those of influence is to have access.

No one wants to be seen as a shameless self-promoter in a crowd, but if you're "networking," that's cool and acceptable. When looking for a job, having breakfast with a bunch of other unemployed people is not a depressing job fair, it's "networking." In fact, many of us no longer have a group of personal friends or even a Christmas card list. We have a "network" of connections and connectors.

The dictionary says a network is an interconnected system of things or people. In the body of Christ, we're not just connected because of a system, but because we are people of covenant. We don't follow a philosophy or a system of thought. We follow a Man. His name is Jesus.

So because we are people of covenant, our network is a brotherhood. *We are allies.*

There is an old expression, "blood is thicker than water." What that has come to mean over hundreds of years is that people born of the same family are closer than outsiders and friendships. But for people of covenant, there is a higher meaning. It literally means that the bond of two people in blood covenant is stronger than those who have been born of the same birth water.

In every culture in the world, you can find a place of covenant that involves the sharing of blood. "Blood brother" means someone who may be unrelated by birth but who swears loyalty to another.

The covenant we share through the blood of Christ Jesus puts us in a different place entirely. We are not just people of contract, connection, or "networking" the way the world defines it. We are people of covenant. We are pulled together because of the blood of Jesus Christ.

So what is "connecting" for daring men? It's more than a network. It's believers connected by covenant for the cause of Christ and the establishing of His kingdom on the earth.

Here's what covenant looks like. It looks like Ross McGinnis.[42]

Ross McGinnis was from Knox, Pennsylvania. At age nineteen, he was the youngest man in his entire company in Baghdad, Iraq. On December 4, 2006, he was in a vehicle with his platoon when a grenade was thrown into the vehicle. Ross McGinnis was the gunner, the man at the opening of the turret, and located at the easiest place to jump from the vehicle. Instead, he looked at those other men, went straight for the grenade, and jumped on it.

The official record of the event says that the grenade flew past McGinnis and down through the hatch before lodging near the radio. Platoon Sergeant Cedric Thomas, recalls that McGinnis yelled, "Grenade! It's in the truck!"

Thomas said, "I looked out of the corner of my eye. I was crouching down, and I saw him pin it down." McGinnis did this, even though he could have escaped. He had time to jump out of the truck. Thomas said, "He chose not to. He gave his life to save his crew and platoon sergeant. He is a hero. He is a professional. He was an awesome man."

For the saving of the lives of his friends and for the giving up of his own, he earned the Medal of Honor.

Ross McGinnis' father wrote this about his son:

"When the doorbell rang Monday evening, December 4th, about 9:30, I wondered who would be visiting at this hour of the evening. When I walked up to the door and saw two U.S. Army officers standing on the patio, I knew instantly what was happening. This is the way the Army tells the next of kin that a soldier has died.

"At that moment, I felt as if I had slipped off the edge of a cliff and there was nothing to grab onto. Just a second beyond safety falling into hell. If only my life could have ended right then. I couldn't blink myself awake. It wasn't a dream.

"As they made their way into our living room, I rushed into the bedroom and told my wife to get up, we had company and they were going to tell us Ross was dead. I didn't know any other way to say it.

"Ross did not become our hero by dying to save his fellow soldiers from a grenade. He was a hero to us long before he died because he was willing to risk his life to protect the ideals of freedom and justice America represents. He has been recommended for the Medal of Honor. We, as parents, are in no hurry to have our son bestowed this medal. That is not why he gave his life. The lives of four men, who were his brothers, outweighed the value of his one life. It was a matter of simple arithmetic, four means more than one."[43]

Ross McGinnis is the picture of a brother, an ally, a friend, a covenant keeper. That father raised a hero by teaching him that "four means more than one."

To be daring is to be positioned for the heroic. To be a hero is to act in a moment of time, on a need greater than self.

The world is waiting for covenant men like you.

We need heroes.

We need daring men.

Meek and Daring Jesus

The idea of the "meek Jesus" was thrown at me for years as I was growing up, and I didn't like it. It seemed effeminate, weak, and wussy. With the word *meek* was always the word *mild*. Growing up with hard-charging surfers, climbing mountains, and riding dirt bikes, I didn't lean toward hanging out with a guy who was "meek and mild," much less desire to make Him my "God" and "Lord." Why would I want to be like *that?*

The wrong definition ruined my image of Jesus for years. When I got the right definition, then, I wanted to be like *that.* Who wouldn't?

When the Romans trained their warhorses, it was a process that took years. The horses were massive, powerful, and would run through any obstacle. The warhorse won battles. It was fierce and fully under the control of the rider. Wherever the rider said to go, the horse would charge.

If you've been around horses, you know they can be spooked. They can run, buck, or jump at the smallest item in their path—a little varmint, a leaf blowing, the sight of a cloth, or with some horses, seemingly nothing at all. They just spook.

So the warhorse had to be trained. In the face of flying arrows and spears, surrounded by mayhem and slashing swords, the horse had to follow the rider. Exactly where the rider wanted to go, regardless of the obstacle or hindrance, the horse was trained to go.

When Jesus came, He told us that everything we saw Him do, was only what the Father led Him to do (John 8:28). We know what God is like, because Jesus in every situation did exactly what God would do. He was a man under authority, and regardless of conditions, He would go, do, and say exactly as God directed Him.

When the Romans finished training a warhorse, it was ready for battle. When the horse was the powerful, strong, explosive beast of war, ready to fight and win in the midst of mayhem, confusion, and unrelenting danger, in their language, the warhorse was then called "meek."

Daring men will follow *that* meek Jesus!

Turn the Other Cheek

Is that really manly? Even the idea that a man would get slapped on the cheek, isn't that just a little feminine? This doesn't seem to go with the daring man theme, much less a powerful Jesus.

Jesus taught a concept that seemed ill-fitted to the strong men he was mentoring, and seemed to contradict the actions He Himself took in beating up swindlers in the church courtyards.

He said, "But I say, do not resist an evil person! If someone slaps you on the right cheek, offer the other cheek also" (Matthew 5:39, NLT). Let's break this apart.

These words were uttered at a time of terrorist Roman occupation. The Romans were brutal to the Jews. Their policy was to subdue the local people by force and terror so the main army could move on to other battles, leaving only a small force to deal with a cowering population.

To do this, the Romans would herd the people of a village to the center plaza, choose the strongest looking man and secure him in the middle of the crowd. The Roman soldier would face the man, demean his manhood verbally then slap him with an open hand across the cheek. No, this is not what real men do. It was a feminine rebuke to his manhood. A real man would hit with a fist and expect a fight. The Roman soldiers, to embarrass the villager, demean his masculinity, degrade his strength and position, would slap him like a girl.

The man had a choice, both of which were the desired result for the soldiers. The man would fight back and they would kill him on the spot, proving their strength over the village. Or, he would back off in retreat. Then the village knew they had no hero to fight for them. It was over.

Jesus brought a fresh, powerful alternative. When they hit, don't cower or fight back. Stand there like a man—strong, resolute with an inner power—and then calmly turn the other cheek, exposing the bully and daring him, "Here, hit this cheek too."

Daring is a strong core of faith with an outward expression of peace.

No man shall be able to
stand before you all the days
of your life; as I was with
Moses, so I will be with you.
I will not leave you nor
forsake you.
Be strong and of
good courage.

~ God's encouragement to Joshua
Joshua 1:5, NKJV

DARING MEN ACCEPT THE CHALLENGE

Act Like a Man

We started with this, and now let's look at it in a few Bible translations:

"Be on your guard; stand firm in the faith; be men of courage; be strong" (1 Corinthians 16:13, NIV).

"Keep your eyes open for spiritual danger; stand true to the Lord; act like men; be strong" (TLB).

In this passage are four key ingredients for an overcoming, victorious, cranked up, and powerful life of strength, the real life of a daring man.

To be on your guard is to be focused, aware that you're in a battle. The enemy has you targeted and you must be vigilant. At any moment, he wants to take you out.

Some of this comes with maturing in Christ. In basketball, my sons first dribbled with their heads down, looking at the ball, and not seeing the open player to pass to. As they matured, their heads came up, their vision clear, and there were no surprises.

The apostle Peter enjoins us to be vigilant, because the devil is looking for whom he may devour (1 Peter 5:8).

We cannot trust the flesh to discern spiritual issues.

Paul said we should stand firm, which is to be fully committed. When a surfer is catching a wave, he cannot sort of catch it. He cannot be lazy in attempting to paddle in. He has to commit.

A friend once said, "A woman cannot be a little pregnant. She must be fully committed."

Paul taught, "It is for freedom that Christ has set us free. Stand firm, then, and do not let yourselves be burdened again by a yoke of slavery" (Galatians 5:1, NIV). Being fully committed to Christ will keep us out of the bondage to sin.

We are told to act like a man, to be men of courage. This means having a resolute spirit, one that has a determined course and will not back away.

To determine a course is a nautical term meaning to set your course of action predicated by the destination.

The writer of the Book of Proverbs told us how we could live like men:

> Trust in the LORD with all your heart,
> And lean not on your own understanding;
> In all your ways acknowledge him,
> And He shall direct your paths.
> ~ *Proverbs 3:5–6, NIV*

Once your course is determined, even if the winds blow you off course, you know how to get back on course.

In the world of golf, the best players are those who are able to rescue themselves from bad shots, to course-correct.

Teams of engineers light up enormous tanks of liquid hydrogen to blast a shuttle carrying a half-dozen highly trained occupants and millions of dollars in equipment into deep space. The success of the space shuttle program was one of science's greatest achievements leading into this century. Yet, with all the best minds in the world—the highly educated and trained teams of scientists—the space shuttle has been said to be on course only 3 percent of the time. The rest of the time, 97 percent, the brilliant teams of rocket scientists make constant course corrections.

You will have midcourse corrections. Don't worry about it. Just maintain your focus and your destination.

Jesus said, "Seek first the kingdom of heaven, and all these things will be added to your life" (Matthew 6:33, my paraphrase).

Paul said, "Be strong." This is the heart, the essence of a daring man: he is relentless. We will never quit. We will not be denied, and we will not turn back.

FOCUSED

COMMITTED

DETERMINED

RELENTLESS

Daring Men and Porn

Imago Dei. That's the Latin term for the image of God engrafted in the soul and texture of man. We are beautifully and mysteriously created beings.

God said we are made in His image. It is the beauty of creative thought, the birth of a baby, the grandeur of the mountains, the power of the oceans, and the breeze in the trees that continually reminds us of our connect to Him.

Pornography, the misuse of the images of God's creation, distorts humanity's three-dimensional beauty into a flattened one-dimensional fake. The genuine becomes the forgery.

This poor stewardship over eyes, over vision, is a key battle of our day. Men and women alike struggle to keep ourselves free from the bondage of lustful thinking, the pain of hidden sins, and the depressing weight of addictions. The Word says we fight against the powers of hell itself. But the promise was given by Christ Himself when He said, "In this godless world you will continue to experience difficulties. But take heart! I've conquered the world" (John 16:33, THE MESSAGE).

We must fight for the God-given, guilt-free joy of intimate pleasures, for the expression of pure and unbridled love. This world will struggle against the constraints of righteousness, but it is into the enduring heart of a righteous warrior God gives His blessing and power. It is through the constraints of monogamy and marriage that the daring man exposes his heart to another and fulfills God's first commandment to be fruitful and multiply.

Daring men know the heat of struggling against temptation. They know the agony of defeat and, rising up like David from the ashes of death, continue to press for the victory, joy, and freedom found in being a follower of Jesus Christ.

Daring men discern the real from the fake.

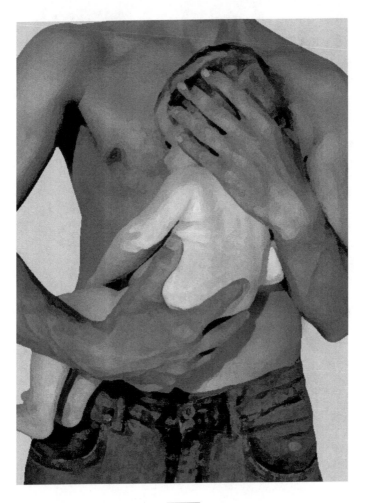

Blind Bart

A blind beggar crouches in doomed expectation of another hopeless day on the road outside Jericho. His name is Bartimaeus. He's the last person you would think of as a daring man.

Bart has been blind since birth. Every day, he squats beside a dust-choked road on a path that, for him, goes nowhere. He has no hope, just a life of begging and dependency on the help of others. Then, he'll die. He seems to be living a life with no meaning.

But then he hears that Jesus of Nazareth is headed that way. Bart's ears perk up. He's heard of Him. Some say He's the Messiah.

People are now crowding into Bart's space on the road. They push him back out of the way, discarded. He's a comma in the paragraph of life, overlooked and passed by.

But there's more to blind Bart than what meets the eye. He sees what those with sight do not. Bart sees opportunity!

Bart stands, facing the noisiest part of the crowd and yells out, "Son of David, Jesus, have mercy on me!" He doesn't call out for Jesus of Nazareth. He calls out for the "Son of David," which the Jews know is the name for the Messiah. This is a discerning act of faith and a daring thing to say in public. He doesn't know if rabbis and Pharisees are standing nearby who could multiply the sorrow of his life exponentially.

People try to quiet him, pull at him, shush him, and push him behind them. Some say, "Don't bother the famous teacher. Who are you anyway?"

"Son of David, JESUS! Have mercy on me!" He's louder. People are more upset. Parents pull their children away from the raving man. Someone looks for the police, motioning to come over and take care of the problem.

Bart knows he has only seconds, not minutes. He screams, "SON OF DAVID, JESUS! HAVE MERCY ON ME!"

Focused, committed, determined, relentless—he's all those.

Then, Jesus stops. Out from the noisy throng, He hears something. It's the call of a daring man using the voice of faith. Jesus recognizes the sound. It captures His attention.

Jesus calls toward the voice and instructs those around him, "Tell him to come here."

Bart gets up, and throws off his coat. His coat! The coat is the beggar's coat. It's his past, his identity. It's how people have known him for years. The coat is his defined being, and HE TAKES IT OFF.

Guided to Jesus, he kneels. Jesus asks him, "What do you want?" Faith is always a specific vehicle. Bart asks for his eyesight.

He leaves healed, a new person, and full of hope, future, and vision.

Desperate people always reach the heart of God.

God responds to the passionate pursuit.

Jesus knows the sound of a daring man calling Him with the voice of faith.

God's Promise to Daring Men

The following passage holds a key covenant from God to us:

> *For He [God] Himself has said, I will not in any way fail you nor give you up nor leave you without support. I will not, I* ***will not, I will not in any degree leave you helpless nor forsake nor let you down*** *(relax My hold on you)! Assuredly not!*
>
> *So we take comfort and are encouraged and confidently and boldly say, The Lord is my Helper; I will not be seized with alarm I will not fear or dread or be terrified. What can man do to me?*
>
> ~ *Hebrews 13:5–6,* AMP

Let's look deeper into this passage. God's covenant with us is: "I will not!" The Amplified Bible translation helps us understand the significance. The original words used by the writer were words of covenant, God giving His word, His promise. When people in early cultures would strike a covenant, they would repeat it in front of witnesses three times. Most Bible translations have this written one time, "I will not." The Amplified translation has it the original way, three times.

With Himself as the witness, God uses a word that does not *imply* a legal contract, but it *is* a legally-binding contract. He wrote it to us, "I will not, I will not, I will NOT." *It is a covenant!*

God Almighty has given His word. He's made covenant with us.

The writer then tells us that because of the promise of God—because it is legally binding and irrefutable—*I can be daring!* God has my back. I can boldly declare in front of the entire world, without hesitation, and with total confidence, "The LORD is my helper! The LORD is my helper! THE LORD IS MY HELPER!"

Say it out loud! Shout the declaration of a warrior, "THE LORD IS MY HELPER! I am not backing down, letting go, or slowing up. I am not going to be lost at sea, ignored when I try and criticized when I fail. Assuredly NOT!"

Wow, what a strong statement—full of courage, daring, endurance, and power: "THE LORD IS MY HELPER!"

Now, go dare to do something that moves you toward your goal. Right now. Go.

A Baseball

It's just a Little League baseball, a bit scuffed up, covered by the scrawled signatures of boys, but it's one of my prized possessions. It was given to me at the close of a season when I had coached a youth baseball team.

It represented dozens of hot, windy, and dusty days and evenings in the north Texas heat. I don't know what our record was that summer. We lost some, won some, had fun, got frustrated at errant throws, laughed at goofy boy stuff, picked up piles of lost clothes, and bonded.

The ball is significant because one of the signatures reads, "Brandon Cole," another, "Bryce Cole"—my sons.

My travel and business were pressing and constant as they grew up. My father had been taught by his mentors to forsake all, including the pleasure of family, for the sake of the gospel. They were wrong. As I played many sports from fourth grade through college—baseball, football, basketball and more—my dad came to perhaps five of my games.

It's just the way it was. Watching my dad's regret, I determined I would not do that with my kids. So, I put my children's activity schedule into the same calendar where I put my business schedule. They had the same priority as my biggest client. I would move what I could to get to their games, plays, and parties.

Today, my little boys are strong men and I'm proud of them. They are building powerful lives of grace, talent, and character. They are amazing in ministry, full of healing and love. They astound me.

Be a dad. You don't have to be amazing. Just be there.

Daring men accept the challenge to be a dad.

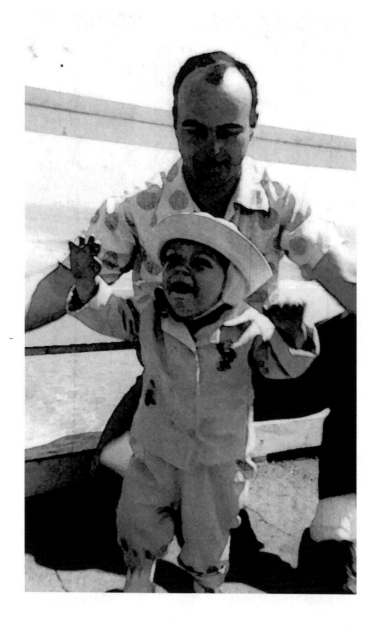

Dad's Daring Challenge

Somehow, it completed the circle. The last memory of touching my dad is the bristled, scratchy feel of his beard as I leaned down to kiss him goodbye. Then, he left. It completed our circle of life because my identity was formed in the closeness of his face to mine when I was a young boy.

A man's identity is shaped in the breath of his father.

Our last moments, our last words, our last communion, our last conversation. While over fifty years of life spanned our experience together as a son and a father, it is the last moments that linger with a bittersweet taste even years after his passing.

I often think of that last conversation after communion with my sisters and friends at Dad's house. Resting in his bed, he talked about Mom, how great life had been, and my daughter's impending wedding. As he struggled to get comfortable, we talked about meaningful things. The time was not given to the frivolous. Our moments were too few, too precious. We spoke about the ministry to men that had wonderfully consumed the latter years of his life, his God-given place of fulfillment.

We spoke of victories past and recent, of special friends, and the incredible privilege of personally knowing so many great men. I leaned down, hugged and kissed his face, and we embraced. As I rose, he grabbed my hand and said, "Are you gonna keep it going?"

He wanted to know about the ministry to men. I had just planted my first church after years in media and thought I'd already been thrown into the deep end by God. So I squeezed his hand and said, "Dad, what you started is in the hearts of great men around the world. It can't be stopped. It's in my heart and the hearts of your grandsons. We will never quit. Don't worry. It will be bigger and stronger. It will happen."

He let go of my hand, dropped deeply back into his pillow and simply said, "Good." Our last conversation, the last words from my dad.

Dad taught me to create the world I would live in, on purpose. "Don't let others create your world for you. For if you do, they will always create it too small," he said.

He taught me that men must be intimately involved in each other's lives and that the key to discipling men is to learn to be vulnerable. He taught me that too many men want to preach sermons behind the safety of a pulpit, but sermons won't change the world. Teaching men truth will change a man's heart, and that will change the world. He taught me to commit to truth and to love the Word.

My life is made up of the things that came out of Dad's heart, the words of his spirit, and the prayers of my Mom. I was blessed to know the love of wonderful parents, to feel the warmth of a father's embrace, and the smile of a Dad who was proud of his kids.

I was blessed to find my identity in the breath of his love.

God's breath is on every man who dares. Your identity is shaped by getting close enough to feel His breath.

DARING MEN ACCEPT THE CHALLENGE

I can still feel Dad's beard on my face. You may have never known that feeling, but you can still stand with me and be my brother.

Stand with me in Ed Cole's last challenge. "Are you gonna keep it going?"

And I ask you the same question as you flip to the end and close this book: *"Are you gonna keep it going?"*

Let me know you're in.

Your brother, friend and ally,

Paul

APPENDIX A

Resources

For your workout, here are some websites that have helped me and a lot of guys. Plus, you can listen to me, too!

Pastor Phil Pringle – www.ccc.org.au

Dr. Jack Hayford –www.jackhayford.org

Andrew Wommack – www.awmi.net

Andy Stanley – www.northpoint.org/podcasts

Christian Mens Network – www.CMN.men

Paul Cole – www.PaulLouisCole.com

Facebook: PaulLouisCole

Twitter: PaulLouisCole

APPENDIX B

Prayers

A Prayer to Become God's Daring Man of Courage

You may not be sure if you're on track yet to be one of God's kind of daring men. The place you start is with a confession that you've messed up in the past and want to do it right now. You make an admission that you need forgiveness for your past and power to change your future. The only One big enough to forgive you is God, and He does it because He sent His Son to die, so you can live. So, now, be daring—*pray this prayer!* Then, what should you expect after you do? Just follow the steps you read in this book, pray every single day and get with some godly men in a local church.

You can be like the daring friends I know around the world who have changed the direction of nations, saved entire generations from life-threatening diseases, fed millions, impacted the future of millions of families—they've been shot at, slandered, imprisoned, had their families threatened, and been betrayed by people around them. But none of them would trade the highs to avoid the lows!

As a committed follower of Jesus I've lived one of the most exciting lives I can imagine—being in places from revolutions in Latin jungles to terrorist firefights in the Middle East, from meeting the famous and powerful leaders of the world to holding the hands of dying AIDS children in Africa... It's been the adventurous path of life God has laid out for me and He has one for you, too.

When I dared to follow, He dared to lead to ever more exciting places. So get started! Say this prayer out loud:

FATHER! In the Name of Your Son Jesus, I admit I've lived less than a daring life. I've messed up, made mistakes, wasted time, sinned against both You and myself, hurt people, and made a mess of things. Do I need You in my life? Yes! Please forgive me. I ask Jesus to move into my life, forgive me for my sins, and fill me with Your Spirit, Your grace, Your power to live the life of a daring man. Thank you for forgiving me. Thank you for helping me to take the next important steps to live for Christ and pursue the daring life You have mapped out for me.

I commit my life to you God, and I thank you for accepting me, right now. Amen.

A Prayer for Sons and Daughters

A lot of men are struggling with their fatherhood. Here's a prayer for your sons and daughters to help you:

Father, in the name of Jesus, we thank You that You have never given up on our children. Father, we thank You that You have never given up on that precious daughter. You have never taken Your eye off that son. Father, I thank You for the next generation. Thank You that our children are marked. Thank You that they have the imprint of Christ on their hearts.

Thank You that our sons and daughters—no matter where they are today or how society is taking advantage of them—they are your children, and God we rescue them now in prayer. We will never let go of them. Father, we thank you that they're on their way back. We thank

You that the prodigal came back. We thank You that the holy hound of heaven is after our children.

In faith, we pray for the next generation, that You will raise up a mighty group of men and women, raise up the warriors, raise up the heroes - raise up daring men and women and may my child be one of them!

I humbly and thankfully pray these things in the name of Jesus. Amen.

NOTES

1. *Lord of the Rings: The Return of the King*, directed by Peter Jackson (2003; n.p.: New Line Home Video, 2004), http://www.imdb.com/title/tt0167260/quotes (accessed September 23, 2010).
2. *The Rise of Theodore Roosevelt*, Edmund Morris, Random House Publishing, 2001
3. Labor Quotations, BrainyQuote.com, http://www.brainyquote.com/words/la/labor183011.html (accessed September 23, 2010).
4. Andrew Jackson Quotes, BrainyQuote.com, http://www.brainyquote.com/quotes/quotes/a/andrew jack122499.html (accessed September 23, 2010).
5. Lance Armstrong Quotes, ThinkExist.com, http://thinkexist.com/quotation/pain_is_temporary-it_may_last_a_minute-or_an_hour/346310.html (accessed September 23, 2010).
6. *Courage*, Edwin Louis Cole, reprinted by Watercolor Books, 2009
7. Theodore Roosevelt, "Citizenship in a Republic," Speech at the Sorbonne, Paris, April 23, 1910, http://www.theodoreroosevelt.org/life/quotes.htm (accessed September 23, 2010).
8. An ancient Scottish saying as told by Lorne Tebutt.
9. Martin Luther Quotes, BrainyQuote.com, http://www.brainyquote.com/quotes/quotes/m/martinluth151409.html (accessed September 23, 2010).
10. Helen Keller Quotes, BrainyQuote.com, http://www.brainyquote.com/quotes/quotes/h/helenkelle121787.html (accessed September 23, 2010).
11. *The Rise of Theodore Roosevelt*, Edmund Morris
12. Michelangelo quotes http://www.wisdomquotes.com/topics/goals/index2.html (Accessed September 24, 2010).
13. *The Truman Show*, DVD, directed by Peter Weir (1998; n.p.: Paramount Home Entertainment, 1999).
14. *You The Leader*, Pax Ministries, 2003, Phil Pringle
15. Jim McMahon Quotes, ThinkExist.com, http://thinkexist.com/quotation/yes-risk_taking_is_inherently_failure-prone/225274.html (accessed September 24, 2010).
16. Calvin Coolidge Quotes, ThinkExist.com, http://thinkexist.com/quotation/nothing_in_this_world_can_take_the_place_of/201002.html (September 24, 2010).
17. Satchel Paige Quotes, SatchelPaige.com, http://www.satchelpaige.com/quote2.html (accessed September 24, 2010).
18. *Power Through Prayer*, by Edward. M. Bounds 1835–1913 Reprinted Whitaker House, 1983
19. *The Power of Potential*, Edwin Louis Cole, reprinted by Watercolor Books, 2009
20. Mike Collett-White, "Titanic Sunk by Steering Mistake, Author Says," *Reuters*, September 22, 2010, as quoted by Yahoo! News, http://news.yahoo.com/s/nm/20100922/lf_nm_life/us_britain_titanic_book (accessed September 29, 2010).
21. Winston Churchill Quotes, ThinkExist.com, http://thinkexist.com/quotation/never_yield_to_force-never_yield_to_the/150136.html (accessed September 24, 2010).
22. U.S. Naval Academy, Official History.http://www. usna.edu/ethics/stockdalelbio.htm (accessed September 24, 2010)

23. Kurt Warner.org, ESPN.com (accessed September 24, 2010).
24. Vine's Expository Dictionary of New Testament Words and Smith and Thayer's, public domain.
25. John Wooden Quote, iWise.com, http://www.iwise.com/m4iEO (accessed September 24, 2010).
26. Shackleton Quote, Antarctic-Circle.org, http://www.antarctic-circle.org/advert.htm (accessed September 24, 2010).
27. Sun Tzu, *The Art of War*, reprinted by Oxford University Press, 1971
28. Thoughts on the Business of Life, Forbes.com, http://thoughts.forbes.com/thoughts/business-marcus-aurelius-antoninus-the-true-worth (accessed September 29, 2010).
29. *The Journal of Christopher Columbus*, recounted by biographer Bartolome de las Casas, 1530.
30. *Ends of the Earth*, Suliasi Kurulo, Resolute Books, 2010.
31. Edwin Louis Cole, *Courage*
32. "The Turn From Goat to Hero, in Thomson's Own Words," *New York Times*, August 21, 2010, http://www.nytimes.com/2010/08/22/sports/baseball/22thomson.html (accessed September 24, 2010).
33. Bill Parcells, Wall Street Journal, Dec. 30, 2008.
34. Seth Godin Blog; http://sethgodin.typepad.com/seths_blog/2010/05/but-what-have-you-shipped.html
35. *Teddy Roosevelt, Mornings on Horseback*, David McCullough, Simon and Schuster, 1982
36. *The Church of the Perfect Storm*, Len Sweet, Adingdon Press, 2008.
37. John Wooden, *They Call Me Coach*, McGraw-Hill, 1988
38. Tzu, *The Art of War*
39. Hinge of History references collected from a variety of sources: Rv. John Jackman at http://www.zinzendorf.com/countz.htm; Bill Muehlenberg, Christianity Today Australia, April 30, 2010; Leslie Tarr, Decision Magazine, May 1977; Moravian Theological Seminary, Bethlehem, Pa. "Leading Historical Figures in Moravian Tradition"; Weinlick, John R. *Count Zinzendorf: The Story of His Life and Leadership in the Renewed Moravian Church*. Revised edition. Bethlehem and Winston-Salem: Moravian Church in America, 1984. The standard English-language biography of the renewer of the Moravian Church (1700-1760).; The Moravians and John Wesley, January 1, 1982, Christianity Today Library.com ; The Great Moravian Revival 1727-1927 by Rev. John Greenfield, self published 1927.
40. Calvin Coolidge, "Address at the Unveiling of the Equestrian Statue of Bishop Francis Asbury," Washington, DC, October 15, 1924, http://www.presidency.ucsb.edu/ws/index.php?pid=24170 (accessed September 28, 2010
41. Oral Roberts, *When You See the Invisible, You Can Do the Impossible* (Shippensburg, PA: Destiny Image Publishers, 2002).
42. Ross Andrew McGinnis Specialist, United States Army, Arlington National Cemetary Website, http://www.arlingtoncemetery.net/ramcginnis.htm (accessed September 28, 2010).
43. Ibid.

BUILDING STRONG MEN

A man that becomes a "real man" will influence his entire family to become faithful members of a local church in more than 90 percent of families. For more than 30 years, MAJORING IN MEN® training has equipped men to become "real." Nearly two million men in more than 100 nations and 80 languages have become "maximized" in their manhood through this simple yet effective outreach to men.

Start MAJORING IN MEN® curriculum and join one of the largest networks of men in the world with:

- Results-oriented training
- A time-tested track record
- Step-by-step process of success for lay leaders
- A global network of ministry resources
- Local church growth through multiplication of men

Join men around the world who are using MAJORING IN MEN® curriculum!

Pastor Michael Murphy, Sydney: "By far the best, most practical and powerful teaching series for men in the world today. We can plant more churches if we'll disciple more men!"

Pastor Joel Brooks, Michigan: "This curriculum will help any church raise faithful men. It's the reason I'm in ministry today!"

Start by studying a Leadership Kit, or the "MAXTrak" books and workbooks or get one of each book Dr. Cole wrote for your library. Whatever you do, start TODAY!

MAJORINGINMEN.com

CHRISTIAN MEN'S NETWORK

For more than 30 years, the ministry of Edwin Louis Cole, Christian Men's Network, has fought the battle for men. To host a men's event in your area or at your church, to launch MAJORING IN MEN® training in your area or at your church or to receive additional information about men's ministry, you may contact Christian Men's Network.

www.CMN.men

ABOUT THE AUTHOR

Paul Louis Cole, DTh, president of Christian Men's Network, is a communicator, church planter, pastor, author, and one of the world's leading experts on men's issues. Paul is an award-winning media writer/producer/director, but his passion is in carrying the message of Christlike manhood globally. The son of Edwin Louis Cole, he has continued the work of the Christian Men's Network, helping pastors build strong men, strong families, and strong churches in over 100 nations. Paul's mission is to rescue men, defeat fatherlessness, and end child abuse by providing leadership tools and strategies to bring a clear and defining word to men.

Paul and his wife of forty-plus years, Judi, reside in Grapevine, Texas. They have three children and five grandchildren.

Christian Men's Network
P.O. Box 3
Grapevine, TX 76092
www.CMN.men

WHO IS READING *DARING*

From a father to a son, he passes the baton and the son goes further than the father ever could....that is the true purpose of a legacy. Paul's book is the exceptional blend of straight talk and scripture to *wake men up*.

~ Glenn Bollinger
President, Alliance Sports Group, Dallas

In *DARING: A Call to Courageous Manhood*, Paul Louis Cole carries on the teachings of his father, my dear friend and mentor, Edwin Louis Cole. *DARING* reawakened my awareness of the daring and dedication of historical Christians. *DARING* reminds us not to quit, and to connect. Every man *and* woman should read this book!

~ Gavin MacLeod
Actor, California

As I read through this book, I wanted to shout, "Reviresco!" a battle term used by the Scottish MacEwen clan meaning, "We shall rise again!" May Paul Cole's call to courageous manhood resonate in your spirit, giving you unflinching resolve to walk in your destiny. Be a man because Jesus became a Man for you!

~ Doug Stringer
Founder/President, Somebody Cares America, Houston, TX

Paul Louis Cole is one of the most influential men of the men's movement today. He is like Joshua that grew up under Moses, strong and courageous! When Paul speaks, men listen because he is the voice of reason for men and it is heard worldwide.

~ Chuck Brewster
President, Champions of Honor, Florida

This book is phenomenal, really phenomenal! Paul's influence has had a profound impact on my life. Paul's newest book, *DARING* is one of the most powerful books to date on manhood. If ever we needed a generation of daring men who will walk in the courage to truly be men, it is now. Every leader needs *DARING* in his library, and every man needs it in his life. Every woman needs to read it and learn about what God wants for her man.

~ Mark J. Chironna
The Master's Touch International Church, Orlando

If ever there was a need in our generation, it is the need for men to deliberately step into their manhood. Paul Cole is carrying the mantle of his father in a fresh, new, relevant and powerful way—exemplified in his book, *"DARING: A Call To Manhood."* Paul's passion is extraordinary and he is speaking to men with a pure anointing that's been tested and tried. He has "a voice" for generations, and if ever there was a time to "lean in" and listen...it is now!

~ Art Sepúlveda
Senior Pastor, Word of Life Christian Center, Honolulu, HIIn this

WHO IS READING *DARING*

In this book, Paul lays out an excellent challenge for men to accept, using scripture and real life examples of manhood. In a society that does not train young men to live courageously, this message is so crucial. I am inspired by Paul's challenge, and I encourage men of all ages to read this book, step up to the plate, and walk in Courageous Manhood.

~ **Ron Luce**
President and Founder, Teen Mania, Texas

I read Paul Cole's book with excitement. It's clear, simple, practical that any man in my church can get their head and hearts around and then be able to act. I loved it. It's time that we "dare" men to act like men and stand up and lead. No one has a greater global ministry in men's ministry that is seeing change by the tens of thousands like Paul Cole - we all have a lot to learn from him.

~ **Bob Roberts, Jr.**
Author *Transformation, Glocalization, Multiplying Church*,
and *Realtime Connections*
Senior Pastor Northwood Church, Keller, Texas

DARING dares to challenge men at our very core, to integrity, character, and to a passionate pursuit of our Lord, and strikes right at the heart of the problem—the unrepentant and selfish heart of man. Are you a real man? Do you want to be a real man? Do you have what it takes to be a real man? If your answer to these questions is "yes," then I DARE YOU to read *DARING*! By the end, you'll know what you have, what you don't have, what you need, and then be challenged to never again settle for where you are!!

~ **Ted DiBiase**
"Million Dollar Man" WWE Wrestler/Hall of Famer, Evangelist,
Mississippi

DONT BUY THIS BOOK!! You could be sorry if you read it. It will make you uncomfortable; challenge you to reevaluate what you really believe; force you to ask some hard questions about yourself, and even life itself. So unless you intend to "man up" and really live life, not just continue with "business as usual"—don't buy this book. On the other hand...

~ **Ben Kinchlow**
Virginia Beach

There are pivotal pages in history that God has used to set the course of Christians worldwide. In his latest book, *DARING*, Paul Cole has prepared such a powerful resource that will shape the thinking of biblical manhood for generations to come. Be sure to read it, receive it and reap a supernatural harvest for years to come. Every dad should give his son a copy and every son should get one for his dad. *DARING* is a man-thing!"

~ **James O. Davis**
President, Cutting Edge International, Florida
Cofounder, Billion Soul Network